LEHI'S DREAM

CHRIST HEALING BY THE WELL OF BETHESDA

LEARNING
IN THE
LIGHT *of* TRUTH

LEARNING
IN THE
LIGHT *of* TRUTH

MERRILL J. BATEMAN

DESERET
BOOK

SALT LAKE CITY, UTAH

Interior photographs by Mark Philbrick, used by permission of BYU.

Library of Congress Cataloging-in-Publication Data

Bateman, Merrill J.
    Learning in the light of truth / Merrill J. Bateman.
        p. cm.
    Includes bibliographical references and index.
    ISBN 1-59038-537-3 (hardbound : alk. paper)
    1. Christian life—Mormon authors. 2. Church of Jesus Christ of
Latter-day Saints—Education. I. Title.
    BX8695.B35A5 2005
    230'.9332—dc22   2005022079

Printed in the United States of America   72076
Publishers Printing, Salt Lake City, UT

10   9   8   7   6   5   4   3   2   1

For Marilyn and the children

CONTENTS

Preface ix

BRIGHAM YOUNG UNIVERSITY—
ITS PAST, PRESENT, AND FUTURE

Prologue—Inauguration Response 3

1. A Zion University 13

2. A Zion University and the Search for Truth 29

3. Children of the Covenant 45

4. From Pioneer Roots to a World-Class,

   Worldwide Institution 55

5. A Peculiar Treasure 81

FAITH, HOPE, AND CHARITY

6. A Faith That Preserves and Strengthens 97

7. Blessings of a Testimony 109

8. Christ Is the Reason 121

9. Hope for Peace 139

CONTENTS

LEARNING IN THE LIGHT OF TRUTH

10. Light, Visions, and Dreams 145

11. "How Knoweth This Man Letters" 155

12. Temples of Learning 171

THE GOSPEL OF JESUS CHRIST

13. One by One 185

14. The Eternal Family 195

15. Lay Hold upon Every Good Thing 209

16. Mortality and Our Eternal Journey 225

LOOKING FORWARD

17. The Dawn of a New Millennium 241

18. The Challenges of the 21st Century 253

Epilogue—Farewell Address 259

Index 263

PREFACE

SOON AFTER President Gordon B. Hinckley announced that I would be the eleventh president of Brigham Young University, President James E. Faust extended an invitation to attend a university function at which he would be the speaker. During the speech, he stated: "Brigham Young University is a continuing experiment as to whether a university whose board of trustees comprises prophets, seers, and revelators can remain a first-class university and not become secularized." The statement was a surprise. I was aware of the secularization that had occurred in almost all of the great universities initially founded on religious principles. But my earlier experiences at BYU had led me to believe that the BYU community understood and believed in the university's divine mission. My initial reaction was: "Of course the test will be successful! The sacred and the secular have coexisted on this campus for more than 120 years." But these thoughts were followed by an impression that I should not take lightly the warning of one of the Lord's prophets.

In the months that followed, a number of conversations, newspaper articles, and events taught me that BYU's divine mission is always at risk. Society in general assumes a secular role for academic institutions. Universities that attempt to integrate the spiritual with the intellectual are considered an oddity in today's world. Academic training for faculty, including BYU's, occurs at secular universities. Further, faculty, staff, and student turnover is considerable. A full understanding and commitment to the university's divine mission is not a given. The special role of the university in the Lord's kingdom should be a frequent topic of discussion. Consequently, several addresses given at devotionals and other settings were devoted to this purpose.

The book begins with the "Inauguration Response" given four months after assuming the presidency—my second major address to the BYU community. A key point of the speech was to provide a vision of the university's future. I had learned of a prophetic statement by President John Taylor in which he said: "You will see the day that Zion will be as far ahead of the outside world in everything pertaining to learning of every kind as we are to-day in regard to religious matters."[1] If that is Zion's destiny, it is certainly the university's as well. Brigham Young University's destiny is to become a Zion university, an extraordinary academic institution within a context of faith. Over time, I learned that the university was making significant progress toward this goal.

The inaugural speech outlines two concerns facing the university and its ability to fulfill its destiny. The first was that given the fixed size of the student body, proportionately fewer and fewer Church members were receiving direct benefits from BYU. A number of conversations with Church leaders across the world indicated that they questioned the value of BYU since few of their members could attend. Those conversations suggested that the university would become less and less important in the Lord's kingdom unless it became more creative in extending the blessings of a BYU education to more Church members. Eventually, this was achieved in three ways under the direction of the board. The first was the initiation of an open enrollment program for spring and summer terms; the second was the creation of more than 400 online courses which currently service more than 100,000 individuals in 40 countries; and the third was the development of BYU Television, which is now available to 35 million households in the United States and a growing audience internationally.

The second concern dealt with the impact of moral relativism that had spread through higher education in the previous four decades. This theory holds that there are no absolute truths—that all truth is relative and circumstantial. The theory has become the foundation for a number of intellectual disciplines. Various forms of the theory undercut the basis for moral and intellectual integrity. It turns secularism into a creed that is no longer neutral but hostile to religion.

During the 1990s, moral relativists were constantly questioning the legitimacy of the university's educational process given the religious connection. Did academic freedom really exist if the pursuit of academic knowledge was circumscribed by a framework of revealed truth? These criticisms demonstrated the need for a clear understanding by the university community of its mission and the university's relationship to the Church. The university's identity had been defined by prophets and seers whose vision was much clearer than that held by the outside world.

The first section of the book groups those addresses that describe the vision of BYU's founding fathers regarding the university's destiny and then outlines what I saw as the future. The first address to the university community is entitled "A Zion University." One commentator called it "unusual" in that it did not lay out "administrative objectives, enrollment goals, and curricula changes, . . . [but] missionary work, miracles, and building Zion." The writer notes that the talk was more than five minutes old before it mentioned the words *Brigham Young University.* But the writer then states: "But in reality, he had been talking about BYU all along. . . . When [he] spoke of the 'kingdom,' it was a sure bet that he also meant BYU. And in any mention of BYU, the kingdom was implied. The two were never separate in his mind. Nor were often dichotomous subjects like secular and spiritual learning and teaching and research."[2]

The theme of the second section of the book is faith, hope, and charity. During my first year as a General Authority, I was asked to assist Elder Neal A. Maxwell in a presentation on faith to the body of the General Authorities. In preparing the material, it became clear that faith is not only a principle of trust but a process for learning. The elements of the process are belief, a willingness to act on the belief, and a witness that what is learned is true. The acquisition of knowledge, whether sacred or secular, follows these steps. In a secular world, a belief that one can gain new knowledge drives the process. The second step is the application of one's mental powers. The third is the understanding that comes with the discovery of a new truth.

The search for sacred truths follows the same pattern. As Alma states, it begins with a "desire to believe" (Alma 32:27). This is followed with diligent application of one's mental powers coupled with obedience to God's commandments—"plant[ing] the seed" (Alma 32:33). The final step is an enlarged understanding, an enlightenment that the principle is true.

The fundamental doctrines of the gospel do not circumscribe or limit the search for truth but open the way for truth to be discovered. The first principle of faith, especially, provides a foundation for the discovery of truth whether sacred or secular. Students who understand this principle accelerate their learning in both realms.

"Hope for Peace" was given on September 11, 2001. A different address had been planned, but as the events of that momentous morning unfolded, it became evident that another topic should be addressed. The incredulity of airliners crashing into the twin towers in New York and the Pentagon pointed to the arrival of a new day—a day when peace in the civilized world was threatened by terrorists who "carry on the secret work of murder" through "secret combinations . . . established in the more settled parts of the land" (Helaman 2:4; 3:23). The first part of the speech assures the students of their safety. The second asks them to be respectful of all people. Other catastrophes had taught a lesson of not speculating and placing blame prematurely. Finally, the most important statement to be made was that the gospel of Jesus Christ is a gospel of peace and life. Only through the gospel can one find peace. Only through the gospel can one be saved from death.

The third section of the book focuses on light and the learning process. The first address discusses the relationship between natural light and spiritual light. In 1884, President Charles W. Penrose noted that physical light and spiritual light belong to one continuum. Just as physical light has a spectrum so does spiritual light with the latter a more refined version of the first. The Light of Christ, near the top of the spectrum, is the source of truth. It is the "Light of Truth." The Lord told Joseph Smith that the restoration of the gospel would be but a beginning to the light that He would pour out upon the earth—both spiritual and temporal (see D&C 121:26–32). The discoveries and inventions of the last 185 years is strong evidence of that outpouring.

The address on "How Knoweth This Man Letters" discusses the learning process followed by the Savior and how it is a pattern for us. He was attentive to His early teachers, Joseph and Mary.

He was a student of the scriptures. Prayer was a daily instrument used to access light. His life was one of application and service. The address points out how the scriptures are a source of light. The scriptures represent "living water" from the Father and the Son. Those who drink deeply will eventually experience a "fulness of joy" (D&C 93:33).

The next section of the book is concerned with various aspects of the gospel of Jesus Christ. "One by One" describes the Lord's interest in and commitment to each person. Just as He invited the multitude to approach Him "one by one" and feel the wounds in His hands, feet, and side, so He guides us individually through the Holy Ghost to experience His saving truths and ordinances. The gospel plan calls for each individual to receive his or her own witness. Testimony is an individual matter. The saving ordinances are administered one by one. The Lord's Atonement is not only infinite, but *intimate,* in that He knows each person and tutors accordingly.

The formation of an eternal family is one of the three great purposes of mortality. Men and women are created as complements (see 1 Corinthians 11:11). They complete each other through marriage and the work of creating a family. Men and women have different strengths, and marriage is meant to be a synergistic relationship in which spiritual growth is enhanced because of the differences.

"Lay Hold upon Every Good Thing" was scheduled for September 11, 2001. Given the events of that morning, this address was delayed one week. "Lay Hold" implores the reader to understand the importance of the eternal family and to do what is necessary to create one. Honor one's parents, discipline one's appetites, provide leadership for younger siblings, be true to one's companion, and nurture one's children. Never give up on the family! Families are welded together through covenants and through love and service.

The final section of the book is concerned with the passing of a century and a millennium and the beginning of a new. It was a privilege to lead Brigham Young University at this point in its history. There was a renewed sense of hope and heightened expectations as one contemplated what the years ahead might hold for BYU, for the Church, and for the world. The explosion of learning and the flowering of science that have taken place in the last two centuries have provided an incredible foundation for future creativity and learning. The "times of refreshing" (Acts 3:19) will continue until the earth is prepared for the Second Coming of the Lord. There is still much knowledge to be revealed and work to be done—both temporally and spiritually. The advancements in transportation, communications, and medicine are but the beginning. One of the critical foundational elements for progress is political freedom which continues to increase across the globe in spite of terrorism.

The sabotaged airliners crashing into the World Trade Center and the Pentagon in 2001 did not fracture the American will or produce a crushing fear in the hearts of people because our common beliefs were a unifying force that provided strength to carry on. As the principles of freedom unite America, so a common faith unites the Latter-day Saint community and, especially, Brigham Young University. There is a force far beyond individual strengths that defines the institution as part of the Lord's kingdom and an integral part of His Church. The university will be an important part of the Lord's work in the years ahead.

I thank everyone who played a part in building the university during my stay. I am grateful for the vice presidents, deans, department heads, and faculty members. They have a vision of

BYU's destiny. I am grateful for the students. They are the heart of the university as they provide the heartbeat. I particularly thank my wife, Marilyn, who stood by my side during both difficult times and good days. She is faithful in all her doings, both to the Lord and to me. She has devoted her energies to building our family. Her sacrifices have nurtured the seeds of our mortality and produced a wonderful garden. Marilyn also contributed to this work in that a few of her devotional addresses were an integral part of my presentations. In those instances, her words have been included. Again, I thank her.

I am particularly grateful to the First Presidency for the trust placed in me and for the many opportunities to learn from them. I thank them also for their permission to publish this work.

I also appreciate the help received from Reid Neilson who provided the impetus for this work by pulling together and organizing the speeches. Thanks go also to Cory Maxwell and to the editors, designers, and typesetters at Deseret Book for turning these pages into a book.

NOTES

1. John Taylor, in *Journal of Discourses*, 26 vols. (Liverpool: F. D. Richards, 1855–86), 21:100, 13 April 1879.

2. Peter B. Gardner, "Striving for Zion," *BYU Magazine*, Summer 2003, p. 30.

Dedication of Joseph Smith statue in courtyard of
Joseph Smith Building, October 17, 1995

First Presidency press conference announcing
new president of BYU, November 2, 1995

BYU devotional,
January 1996

President and Sister Bateman with President
Gordon B. Hinckley and President Thomas S.
Monson at BYU commencement, Bateman
inauguration, April 1996

President and Sister Bateman at devotional with
President Thomas S. Monson,
March 11, 1997

BYU Commencement with President
Thomas S. Monson and President
James E. Faust in attendance, August
1997

Islamic translation meeting
with Ambassador Muasher
of Jordan, February 3,
1998

Islamic translation dinner, Los Angeles,
California, Daniel Peterson, Merrill J.
Bateman, Elder Jeffrey R. Holland, and
guest, February 11, 1998

"Lighting the Way" campaign filming, Squaw Peak, August 13, 1999

President Bateman conferring honorary doctorate on Sister Marjorie Hinckley, BYU Commencement, April 20, 2000

President Hinckley honoring LaVell Edwards at Coach Edwards' last home game, November 18, 2000

Unveiling of Carl Bloch's painting, "Christ Healing by the Well of Bethesda," December 4, 2001

Commencement, April 25, 2002

President Bateman greeting new graduate at reception ceremony, April 25, 2002

Devotional, January 13, 2003

Sister Bateman speaking to a group of students, May 15, 2003

Brigham Young University—

Its Past, Present, and Future

Inauguration Response

(25 APRIL 1996)

TODAY, I HAVE taken a most solemn oath to preserve, protect, and defend Brigham Young University. The kingdom is unique—and so is this institution, which is an integral part of it.

The latter-day cords of faith stretch from a grove of trees in Palmyra to a jail in Carthage, from Carthage to the Great Salt Lake, and now from these mountain valleys to 159 nations and territories. The destiny of the kingdom is to be in and among all nations, kindred, tongues, and people. Graduates of Brigham Young University are part of that destiny.

An Ending and a Beginning

Thank you for letting me share this day. It is unusual to combine an inauguration with a commencement. A presidential inauguration usually occurs within three to four months of the appointment. Also, it is scheduled at a time when faculty, staff, and students are able to attend. Rather than scheduling two major university events back-to-back, a decision was made to combine your ending here with my beginning. Please consider this event as symbolic in that every ending is a beginning. You complete a major step today and begin another phase where you as adults enter a new world prepared to serve.

Today's event is a reminder of another ending. Little more than one month ago, President Rex E. Lee finished his mortal probation. His untimely death deeply affected this campus. President Lee devoted more than twenty years of his life to Brigham Young University as student body president, founding dean of the Law School, occupant of the George Sutherland Chair of Law—and finally as president. Toward the end of his tenure, he faced increasingly difficult health conditions, including two forms of cancer and pneumonia. In spite of illness, he was determined to serve to the end. May I share with you his last gift to BYU.

President Lee was one of this country's foremost legal advocates. He was an absolute master in the courtroom. On 25 January 1996, Rex Lee argued his last case in the Tenth Circuit Court of Appeals in Denver. The client was Brigham Young University. The American Civil Liberties Union had appealed a lower court loss in a housing case against the university. In spite of President Lee's illness and weakened physical condition, he insisted that he represent BYU before the court. At this time he was confined to a wheelchair and required oxygen. The plane carrying President and Sister Lee and the other members of their party left Salt Lake City on 24 January 1996, after many hours of delay due to a heavy snowstorm. President Lee was totally exhausted and short of oxygen upon his Denver arrival. Eugene Bramhall, the university's general counsel, shared with me the events of the next day:

On the morning of the hearing, Rex and Janet, plus those accompanying them, left the hotel at 9:00 A.M. in the teeth of a blizzard for the two-block walk to the courthouse. It was very cold and Rex was bundled up in a blue overcoat, with one of the attorneys pushing him in the chair. He was frail but cheerful, optimistic, and cracking jokes about the little handcart company on its way to the Tenth Circuit. Upon arriving at the courthouse, Rex's party checked through security, made its way to the second floor, and waited for their case to be called.

The courtroom was full of lawyers and clients [waiting for their cases to be tried]. During the presentation of the ACLU's argument, there was the usual bustle and inattention on the part of everyone except those directly involved. At the conclusion of the appellant's presentation, Rex wheeled himself to the center of the courtroom, adjusted his oxygen bottle on the floor alongside his wheelchair, pulled the microphone on the podium down close to his mouth and said, "Good morning, Your Honors. I am Rex Lee, counsel for Brigham Young University." One or two lawyers who were working on their cases put their notebooks away and began to listen. The argument followed. Rex drew obvious strength from the exchange with the judges. His voice became stronger. He became more animated. There was a chuckle here and a wise observation there. Soon, everyone in the courtroom was watching.

The place became quiet, like a church. The master advocate was at work. His last argument was clear, lucid, direct, and thoughtful and showed a magnificent grasp of the [relevant] cases. It was almost like a sermon. His text was the law, his congregation the court and everyone in the courtroom. His subject was Brigham Young University, his beloved alma mater, and its history, its traditions, its values, its very purpose. Janet had tears in her eyes as perhaps she recognized that there would be few moments left like this one for one so dear to her and one whom she had so fiercely protected for such a long time. Rex gave everything he had to the university for a period of twenty years.[1]

This was his last gift.

Prophecies Coming to Pass

An inauguration ceremony is a time to review the past and declare direction for the future. In reviewing past prophetic statements concerning BYU, I was drawn to one by President John Taylor issued more than one hundred years ago. It relates to the past but also to the present and the future. President Taylor said: "You will see the day that Zion will be as far ahead of the outside world in everything pertaining to learning of every kind as we are to-day in regard to religious matters. You mark my words, and write them down, and see if they do not come to pass."[2] If Zion's destiny is to be far ahead of the outside world in everything pertaining to learning, one would expect its university to lead the way in terms of secular knowledge, with leadership in spiritual matters reserved for the prophets.

At what point in the educational journey is this institution? How far has the university come from its early beginnings? What does the future hold as we look forward one or two decades? One hundred and twenty years ago, Brigham Young Academy was basically a normal school preparing young men and women to teach in the secondary and elementary systems. It had twenty-nine students and one teacher—Karl G. Maeser. It was impoverished and survived the first twenty-one years only through the sacrifices of its faculty, its board of trustees, and the Church. In the twenty-first year of its life, the school was incorporated as a subsidiary of the Church, which then assumed responsibility for its future.[3]

The major period of growth occurred following World War II. Between 1945 and 1970 the university matured physically as the student body grew from 1,500 to 25,000, with all fifty states and more than seventy countries represented in 1970. During the past twenty-five years, the increase in students, faculty, and staff has been modest. Today, there are 27,000 students supported by 5,000 faculty and staff.

But in contrast to the stable population of the last twenty-five years, educational quality accelerated at an exponential rate. Between 1970 and 1995, the average ACT score for entering freshman increased from 23, which was 14 percent above the national norm, to 27, which is 42 percent above the national norm. During the same period, the average high school grade point for the entering class jumped from 3.1 to 3.7. Today BYU ranks tenth among all universities in the number of National Merit scholars who are admitted. Fourteen years ago we were forty-sixth. The ever larger pool of applicants and the enrollment cap pushed the entrance bar higher and higher.

Not only is the student input of high quality, so is the output. Brigham Young University ranks fifth among private universities in the number of undergraduates who earn doctoral degrees. The percentage of BYU applicants accepted in medical and dental schools is 40 percent above the national average. Recently the university ranked twenty-second as a teaching institution when compared with 228 other schools. The J. Reuben Clark Law School is consistently ranked in the top quarter of law schools in the country—an extraordinary accomplishment in its short life. The Marriott School of Management is in the top 10 percent of business schools, and the School of Accountancy is ranked number three in the country by accounting educators. Texas A&M just completed a study that ranks BYU's manufacturing engineering technology program as number one. The university's College Bowl team placed in the top five at the1996 National College Bowl tournament. Quality improvements in faculty and staff have kept pace with the student body. And the large number of BYU graduates earning doctoral degrees at other institutions is our insurance for the future.

Living Up to Our Destiny

The one constant throughout BYU's history is its spiritual commitment. From President Brigham Young's initial charge to Karl G. Maeser to President Thomas S. Monson's charge today, every subject is to be taught with testimony under the direction of the Spirit. The gospel of Jesus Christ is the common denominator at this university and embraces all subjects. Teachers and students understand that all truth is spiritual. Therefore the discovery of secular truth is enhanced by following spiritual truth.

Now, what of the future? First, the spiritual mandate will continue and become even more important as the general society stumbles deeper into spiritual darkness. In the words of Franklin S. Harris, fifth president of BYU:

> The first task of the future is to preserve at the institution this spirit that comes to us from the past—the true

spirit of the Brigham Young University. This spirit places character above learning and indelibly burns into the consciousness of the student the fact that the most enduring joy is dependent on spiritual growth which looks toward eternal progression.[4]

The key to maintaining the distinctive character of Brigham Young University is in the testimonies of the faculty and the staff. A large number will retire in the next few years. They must be replaced by well-prepared candidates who view the world and their disciplines through the gospel lens.

The quality of education at Brigham Young University will continue to increase. Student test scores will rise even higher. The university will soon rank among the top five schools in the number of National Merit scholars that are admitted. The student body will become more international and ethnically diverse as LDS membership increases at home and abroad. More and more faculty will become known nationally and internationally.

In spite of these trends and expected accomplishments, there are two concerns. The first is that proportionately fewer and fewer Church members will benefit from the University. More and more Latter-day Saints will attend college elsewhere. As a partial offset, university processes must be as efficient as possible. We must use the brick and mortar as fully as possible. We must take advantage of new technology where possible. The time it takes to graduate must be shortened, and, even more important, we must become more creative in extending a BYU education to the members of the Church.

The second concern is the moral relativism spreading throughout higher education both in America and abroad. Although higher education was secularized during the past century, there was still faith in reason and knowledge through the 1960s and into the 1970s. Absolute religious truths had been largely rejected by the world long before the 1970s, but scientific absolutes were still in vogue. During the past two decades, however, a number of well-known educators had begun to denigrate truth. In a recent article, Gertrude Himmelfarb states that the driving force was a "radical relativism and skepticism that rejects any idea of truth, knowledge, or objectivity." There is no God. There are no absolute truths—only that which is politically useful. Those associated with this movement "refuse even to aspire" to truth on the basis that it is "unattainable and undesirable"—the latter because the search for truth is assumed to be "authoritarian and repressive" by nature. The politicization of the university that occurred following World War II has allowed the relativist movement to take hold within the university. The premise is "no truth, no facts, no objectivity . . . only will and power." The slogan is "Everything is political."[5] The result is characterized by Dostoyevsky's Ivan Karamazov who said, "If God does not exist, everything is permitted."[6]

If university scholars reject the notion of "truth," there is no basis for intellectual and moral integrity. Secularism becomes a creed that is no longer neutral but hostile to religion. The university becomes a politicized institution that is at the mercy and whims of various interest groups. Tolerance is encouraged unless one's ideas are different. The word "diversity" is becoming a code word for "uniformity." Universities are encouraged to be diverse from within but not from without. A question arises. If the large majority of faculty at a religious university are of the same faith, is there enough internal diversity by the world's standards? For some educators, a religious university is a contradiction in terms.

Where is BYU amidst these transformations in higher

education? Fortunately, the board of trustees is totally committed to the pursuit of academic truth within the framework of revealed truth. Annually, Church leaders reaffirm verbally and with financial support their commitment to higher education and the dual function of the University—"secular learning, the lesser value, and spiritual development, the greater." At BYU the purpose of education is to make men and women whole, both in competence and in conscience.

Finally, I close with a brief story that illustrates BYU's destiny amidst the uncertainty surrounding many other institutions of higher education. Some years ago, three Brigham Young University professors attended a conference at Baylor University entitled "Christian Higher Education—Will It Survive?" Toward the end of the conference, one of the seminars posed the question, "Of the three most prominent religious-based universities—Baylor, Notre Dame, and Brigham Young—which will still be around as a religious institution in fifty years?" During the course of discussion, the editor of a Catholic publication walked by one of the groups that included a BYU faculty member. He stopped to listen to the discussion. Finally, he remarked, "BYU will be the only one to survive because it has not bought into moral relativism."[7]

How ironic—a Catholic editor at a Baptist conference declaring that the Latter-day Saint university would be the only one to keep its religious moorings. I don't know about Notre Dame. I don't know about Baylor. But I pray that what he said about BYU is true, and I pledge all in my power to protect, defend, and preserve the special relationship that it has with the kingdom.

NOTES

1. Eugene Brimhall, Letter, March 1996, in my possession.

2. John Taylor, in *Journal of Discourses,* 26 vols. (Liverpool: F. D. Richards, 1855–86), 21:100, 13 April 1879.

3. See Ernest L. Wilkinson and W. Cleon Skousen, eds., *Brigham Young University: A School of Destiny* (Provo, Utah: Brigham Young University Press, 1976), xi.

4. Franklin S. Harris, "Inaugural Address," in *Educating Zion,* eds. John W. Welch and Don E. Norton (Provo, Utah: BYU Studies, 1996), 8.

5. Gertrude Himmelfarb, "A Call to Counterrevolution," *First Things* 59 (January 1996): 18.

6. See Fyodor Dostoyevsky, *The Brothers Karamazov,* Part 1, Book 2, Chapter 6.

7. Personal conversation with Professor Keith J. Wilson, BYU College of Religion, who attended the seminar, "Contribution to Pluralism," October 20, 1995, Baylor University.

CHAPTER 1

A Zion University

(9 JANUARY 1996)

For many years I have been observing the great miracle the Lord is performing on this earth as He builds a Zion people in country after country. In July 1956 I traveled by train and ship from Salt Lake City to London, England, to begin a mission for the Church. Upon arrival, I learned that approximately 15,000 members lived in Great Britain in fifteen districts. There were no stakes. In fact, the number of stakes in the entire Church totaled only 239, and all but twelve were in the western United States and Canada. Upon completion of the mission two years later, there were sixteen districts in Great Britain but still no concentration of Saints large enough to organize a stake. In 1971 I returned to England as an employee of an American company. A few stakes existed in the British Isles by then, but the bulk of the Saints were still scattered and met in small congregations. My family lived in a tiny branch thirty-five miles west of London. The attendance at our first sacrament meeting was fourteen, including my family of seven. We met in a small schoolhouse with many members driving fifteen or more miles to attend. Twenty-three years have passed since our family returned from England, and the small seeds planted by missionaries and others after World War II have turned into a miraculous harvest. Two years ago I returned to Britain on Church business and learned that more than forty stakes now exist in the British Isles. Membership exceeds 166,000.

Since my call as a General Authority in 1992, I have learned that the British experience is not unique. As late as 1966 there was only one stake in Brazil. On a recent trip to São Paulo, the Area Presidency informed us that the 150th stake would be created by the end of 1995, with Brazilian membership exceeding one-half million. The growth in Chile, Argentina, Peru, Mexico, and the Philippines is similar to that of Brazil. In early 1970 there were no stakes in Japan. Today there are twenty-five. Korea's first stake was created in 1973. Today there are sixteen. In 1978, following the revelation on the priesthood, I was called by Elder James E. Faust, then president of the Church's International Mission, to accompany Elder Ted Cannon on a fact-finding mission through West Africa. Although numerous groups of people in Ghana and Nigeria expressed interest in the Church at the time, total membership was less than one hundred. West African membership today totals more than 70,000, and stakes exist throughout the region.

The prophets Daniel and Isaiah saw this phenomenon happening in the last days. Daniel stated: "And in the days of these kings shall the God of heaven set up a kingdom, which shall never be destroyed: and the kingdom shall not be left to other people, but it shall break in pieces and consume all these kingdoms, and it shall stand for ever" (Daniel 2:44).

Isaiah likened the Church to a tent and said that in the last days it would stretch forth across the earth by lengthening its cords and strengthening its stakes (see Isaiah 54:2).

How is this done? How are people's hearts and minds changed so that conviction and commitment exist in their souls? What role does Brigham Young University play in this marvelous venture? With regard to the transformation occurring in the hearts of men and women, I have learned that the great miracle of the Church is based on thousands and thousands of small, quiet miracles. May I illustrate with two examples.

Four weeks prior to Elder Cannon's and my trip to West Africa in July 1978, fifty letters were sent to members and non-members in the various countries apprising them of our visit and asking them to meet us at the airport upon arrival. During a four-week period we visited eight cities in four countries. With the exception of one city, no one received a letter in time to meet us. Toward the end of the trip, we arrived in Calabar, Nigeria, on a Friday afternoon, needing the services of a previously identified member to help us find approximately fifteen congregations in the southeastern part of the country. Each congregation had adopted the name of our Church, and the leaders had written asking for information and missionaries.

The member, Ime Eduok, was not at the airport or at the hotel. Brother Cannon and I checked in and went to our room, not knowing where or how to find Brother Eduok in a city of one million. The next two days were a critical part of the trip, and Brother Eduok was the only one who could help us. We knelt in prayer and asked the Lord to guide us to him. We returned to the lobby and asked the desk clerk if she knew Mr. Eduok. She did not. Within a few minutes a large number of Nigerians had gathered around us discussing our plight but lacking the information needed. Suddenly, I felt a hand on my shoulder. I turned to see a large man standing next to me who said: "Did I hear you say Ime Eduok? He is my employee. I just entered the hotel to buy a newspaper on my way home from work. Ime will be leaving the firm in fifteen minutes. I do not know where he lives. If he leaves the office before you arrive, it is unlikely that you will find him before Monday." The man hurriedly put us in a taxi and gave the driver directions. We arrived at the business just as Ime Eduok was locking the door. Brother Eduok guided us to each congregation during the Saturday and Sunday that followed. Many people in those congregations are now members of the Church, and information gleaned from them formed an important part of the report given to the First Presidency upon our return.

The second incident comes from a story told by Elder Russell M. Nelson of the Quorum of the Twelve:

> [A] beautiful young mother named Svetlana [living in Leningrad, Russia] had importuned the Lord in prayer to make it possible for her to obtain a Bible written in the Russian language. Such a Bible [was] rare, precious, and very expensive. In the fall of 1989, she and her [family] went to Helsinki in quest [of] a Bible. While walking through a park in Helsinki, she stepped upon an object hidden beneath the ground cover of autumn leaves. She picked it up and found it to be the answer to her prayers. It was a Bible written in the Russian language. So excited was she that she joyfully recounted the story of this great discovery to another mother who was also in the park with her youngster. The second mother then [asked] Svetlana, "Would you like to have *another* book about Jesus Christ, also written in the Russian language?" Svetlana . . . answered in the affirmative.[1]

The Finnish woman, wife of a district president, gave Svetlana a copy of the Book of Mormon and invited her to church. Svetlana took the missionary lessons, joined the Church, and returned to Leningrad with her family. She then invited friends into her home, and many of them responded to the message of the missionaries and were baptized. Svetlana, her friends, and others like them are the pioneer foundation upon which the Church has been built in that part of the world.

Why was a Nigerian with vital information prompted to deviate from his normal course and stop at a hotel to buy a newspaper? How did a rare, expensive Russian Bible find its way into a Finnish park, coincident with the passage of a Russian woman who had been praying for such a book? How did the wife of a Finnish district president just happen to be in the park to share in the joy of the rare prize? Brothers and sisters, who is guiding the Church? We live in a day when hundreds of thousands of small miracles are quietly occurring as the Lord prepares the honest in heart for entrance into His kingdom and the earth for His return. What role does Brigham Young University play in this process? The answer depends on our testimonies and how we view the university in its relationship to the Church.

Apart from or a Part of the Church

Is the university apart from or a part of the Church? Following the announcement of my appointment as president of Brigham Young University, the *Salt Lake Tribune* carried an article on what it means to have a General Authority as the school's leader.[2] The major point of the article concerned the university's relationship to the Church. The news reporter suggested that although some might have assumed prior to the announcement that the university was a secular institution distinct from but reporting to the Church, the call clearly indicates that the university is an integral part of the kingdom. The article surprised me in that I had never thought of Brigham Young University as separate from the Church. Prophet after prophet has stated clearly that Brigham Young University is a religious institution with a divine mission, even though secular education is a key part of its purpose. Given the organizational structure by which the university is governed, it seems paradoxical that some might think that Brigham Young University is not an integral part of The Church of Jesus Christ of Latter-day Saints. The Church itself is an educational institution, and Brigham Young University is one of its key components. Thus, one might say that this institution is not only a university in Zion but is in the process of becoming a "Zion university."

From the very beginning education has been one of the central missions of the Church. The School of the Prophets, established in Kirtland, Ohio, in 1833, foreshadowed the creation of the University of the City of Nauvoo in 1841. The purpose of the Nauvoo school, as stated by the Prophet Joseph Smith and his counselors, was "to teach our children wisdom, to instruct them in all the knowledge and learning, in the arts, sciences, and learned professions. We hope to make this institution one of the great lights of the world, and by and through it to diffuse that kind of knowledge which will be . . . for the public good, and also for private and individual happiness."[3]

The Prophet Joseph's dream to build a university that would become a light to the world was cut short by a mob's bullet on 27 June 1844. But the dream burned deeply inside another prophet. Brigham Young taught, "Ours is a religion of improvement,"[4] and "Every art and science known and studied by the children of men is comprised within the Gospel."[5]

In February 1850, only two and one-half years after the first wagon train entered the Salt Lake Valley, the Latter-day Saints created the University of Deseret, the first institution of higher learning west of the Mississippi and a testimony to the value placed on education by the Saints. Brigham Young University was founded in 1875 by the prophet whose name it bears. It has become the flagship of the Church's educational system. It is becoming the light to the world that Joseph foresaw and through which knowledge is and will be diffused for public good and personal happiness. Let us now explore what it means for Brigham Young University to be a Church entity, a Zion university.

A Zion University

The word *Zion* in Latter-day Saint literature refers to the "pure in heart" or the place where the pure in heart dwell (D&C 97:21; see Moses 7:18–19). A Zion people are of one heart and one mind—they dwell in righteousness and have no poor among them. "The word *university* originally meant a community," but it also is used to mean "cosmos" or "totality."[6] In our context, a Zion university is a community of righteous scholars and students searching for truth for the purpose of educating the whole person. They understand that God's children are more than intellect and body. The intellect is housed in a spirit that must also be educated. Sacred or higher truths relating to the spirit are the foundational truths in a Zion community and center on Jesus Christ as the Son of God, the Only Begotten of the Father in the flesh, the sacrificial Lamb who gave His life for the sins of the world, the First Fruits of the Resurrection. Community members also have full faith in the appearance of the Father and the Son to the Prophet Joseph in a vision in a grove of trees, believe that other angelic visitors also appeared to him, and believe that the gospel and the holy priesthood were restored to earth following a long period of apostasy. They know that the Book of Mormon is what it professes to be and that revelation from God to His prophets is the guiding instrument for the Church.

But we must remember that a university also has a prime obligation to teach secular truth. Our goal is to achieve excellence in this sphere. There must be no alibi for failure to achieve a first-class rank within the parameters set by the board of trustees. Continual improvement of faculty qualifications and performance is the key to this objective.

Because the gospel is the common denominator at this university and since all truth is part of the gospel, every subject must be taught with testimony. Testimony is not to be encased in particular institutions on campus.[7] Brigham Young University is not a Harvard of the West or a Stanford of the Rocky Mountains with an institute of religion on the periphery. We have the opportunity to be better at discovering and teaching truth, all truth, because testimony can be everywhere and permeate everything.[8] Testimony and the Holy Spirit have as much to do with English and mathematics as with religion if we are diligent in scholarship and obedient to gospel principles. Teachers and students in this community should understand that all truth is spiritual, and thus the so-called secular truths may be discovered by revelation as well as by reason.

Arthur Henry King was a great Shakespearean scholar at this university. He understood the process of revelation in the discovery of secular truth. In a BYU forum speech in 1972, he related the following:

Niels Bohr, [the] Danish physicist Nobel-Prize winner
. . . is reported to have said that he owed his discoveries
more than anything else to the reading of Shakespeare.
That may seem odd unless we have read that apparently
frivolous book called *The Double Helix* about the discovery of the form of a genetic molecule by a young
American in Cambridge: he tells exactly what happened
during the days when he progressed towards that discovery. It is worth reading to realize that great discoveries in
science like great writing come ultimately from—call it
what you like—intuition; I would call it inspiration. The
wind apparently "bloweth where it listeth"; but can anything worth-while happen on any university campus with
which the Holy Ghost is not involved?[9]

My favorite story illustrating the role of the Holy Ghost and
the Light of Christ in the discovery of truth comes from James W.
Cannon, a member of our mathematics department, regarding his
discovery of how to unknot an infinitely knotted object in high-
dimensional space. (He was a professor at the University of
Wisconsin at the time.) After pushing the problem around
for many months with no success, the solution came in an
unexpected manner. He records:

One night at 2:00 A.M., my eyes suddenly popped
open. I sat up in bed. . . . I knew how to extend
S(breve)tan'ko's techniques. I do not know how the
answer came to me. I couldn't sleep. I dressed quietly and
went walking on the dark streets of Madison. . . . I
checked the ideas for all of their consequences. I checked
for absurdities. I couldn't find any. The picture was
wonderful.[10]

Brother Cannon's experience is not unusual. After studying, puzzling, and dreaming about a problem, scientists often find progress stopped. Then, suddenly, as if out of nowhere, a flash of light comes. Secular truth is revealed by the Spirit as well as sacred truth.

Faculty Responsibility and Academic Freedom

A Brigham Young University appointment is a sacred trust. More than 27,000 youth of the Church selected on the basis of gospel commitment and scholarship potential are under our stewardship. Consequently, we have a responsibility to nurture their faith and improve their academic skills. The great majority of us are members of The Church of Jesus Christ of Latter-day Saints, and the prime requisite for employment is a personal testimony of and behavior consistent with the restored gospel. Nonmember faculty and staff are expected to live according to the light within them and standards agreed upon at the time of employment.

Placing commitment to gospel truths first in the life of a faculty member does not demean the second requirement of academic excellence. If testimony and high personal standards are the foundation, outstanding scholarship that includes teaching ability is the capstone. Both testimony and scholarship are essential for this university to achieve its destiny. They are not competitive but complementary elements. The desire for excellence covers graduate studies and research in selected areas as well as continued improvement of undergraduate teaching.

A personal commitment to gospel standards by faculty members will increase, not decrease, academic freedom. If applied, the gospel framework will keep us from gathering like flies hovering over the dead carcasses of secular error. As a close faculty friend pointed out to me recently, the greatest limitation on academic freedom comes when faculty take for granted the assumptions of colleagues at other institutions while developing secular theories. We will be more productive and enjoy more freedom if we examine and test secular assumptions under the lamp of gospel truth. We must not blindly accept the choices made by others. These statements obviously apply more to the social sciences and humanities than to the physical sciences, engineering, and the professions. However, even scholars in these areas would do well to measure the worth of their scholarship in the gospel light.

A brief illustration is in order. In speaking of the last days, Isaiah and Nephi indicate that people will "call evil good, and good evil; [will] put darkness for light, and light for darkness; [will] put bitter for sweet, and sweet for bitter!" (Isaiah 5:20; 2 Nephi 15:20). Recently, I learned about a movie that was described by a newspaper critic as "wonderful, joyous." It was rated PG-13. The film features seven illicit relationships, including open marriage, fornication, and adultery. The main messages of the film are first, open marriages are acceptable; second, it is appropriate for men to abandon their wives and families if they become stressed; third, illicit relationships relieve grief and do no harm if secrecy is maintained; and fourth, premarital sex is normal. To a committed Latter-day Saint, the film is not wonderful or joyous but depressing and sad as evil is called good, again and again. There is a stark contrast between the messages of the film and the recently issued proclamation on the family by the First Presidency and the Quorum of the Twelve.[11]

There are scholars in this university who study the family. There are classes taught in several disciplines that relate to the family. If scholarship and teaching at this university are based on the proclamation's standards rather than on the world's standards, academic freedom will increase and students will be spiritually strengthened to withstand the onslaught of evil—theories and practices that the world calls good. A society that is in moral decline is also in intellectual decline; for the one surely follows the other and follows fast.[12]

The grass is not greener on the other side of the fence. What may appear to be limits on academic freedom derived from the religious nature of the institution actually provide additional freedom. It is imperative that we not mimic the research and teaching choices of our colleagues at other universities without first using the measuring rod of the gospel.

I believe, using the Lord's measuring stick, that we have the finest faculty and staff in the world. It is clearly the strongest faculty and staff ever assembled at Brigham Young University. I firmly believe that the Lord will strengthen the faculty in the process of time.

A Message to the Students

May I paraphrase an earlier president of Brigham Young University: "Our reason for *being* is to be a university. But our reason for *being a university* is the students."[13] For more than 120 years this campus has had a distinctive character. Strangers who visit are struck by the cleanliness and orderliness of the buildings, the grounds, and especially the people. Although the Dress and Grooming Standards may not seem as important as other parts of the Honor Code, they help us be a distinctive people. I remember visiting other college campuses during the early 1970s while serving as a faculty member at this university. It was the height of the "hippie" period, when long hair, drug use, sloppy clothes, and rebellion were the order of the day. It was so refreshing to return to this campus, to see the clean young people, and to feel the peace that prevails here.

May I share with you a flash of insight given me by the Spirit twenty years ago in which I learned about this university's major role in building the kingdom. It concerns you, the students. The Bateman family had just returned to Provo from the East Coast following my appointment as dean of the School of Management. We had been away for four years with a multinational corporation and had enjoyed ourselves immensely. Although we knew the decision to return to Brigham Young University was correct because prayers had been answered, I was still struggling emotionally with the new assignment.

In September 1975 we attended the first multi-stake fireside of the school year. We were sitting high up in the Marriott Center near portal C. As the speaker began his sermon for the evening, I looked out across a congregation that must have totaled 18,000, including all of the missionaries from the MTC. They were easy to spot because they were allowed to take off their suit coats! Approximately 2,500 white-shirted missionaries filled the section under portal M, and it was a sea of white. I looked at them and realized that within weeks they would be scattered to the four corners of the globe. It was exciting to contemplate the people they would serve, the change that would occur in the missionaries as they matured spiritually, and the miracles that would bring new members into the Church.

Then a flash of inspiration opened my mind as to the purpose of Brigham Young University. I realized that 27,000 students were being prepared to enter the world. Every year approximately 6,000 would leave Provo, scattering across North America with some going on to Europe, others to Asia, some to Africa, and a number to South America. Some might even go Down Under. If the university performed its roles well, deepening spiritual roots and providing a first-class education, in the course of time strong Church families would grow up in hundreds and thousands of communities all over the world. These BYU families would be waiting when later missionaries arrived. My earlier experiences in London, Boston, Colorado Springs, High Wycombe, Lancaster, Bedminster, Accra, and Lagos had pointed to the importance of just one or two strong families to form a core around which the Lord could build a branch, then a district, and finally a stake. The BYU families would be good neighbors; have strong relationships with business associates; and, if well-trained, be leaders in their communities. These strong families, by example and invitation, would open doors for missionaries to enter.

I then knew why we had returned to Brigham Young University. It provided a satisfying feeling on the journey home that evening. Students leaving the university with a first-rate education combined with spiritual strength based on faith in Christ and His restored gospel have a tremendous advantage in the world. They know who they are. They need not be afraid. Faculty members should know that their teaching and research are building something of great worth. Brigham Young University is a major contributor to the central mission of Christ's kingdom on earth.

This institution will not fail. As Daniel prophesied, the kingdom will not be left to other people. Joseph's and Brigham's vision that the spiritual can be combined with the secular without the latter overcoming the former will prove true because of faith and priesthood power. Brigham Young University will continue to be a light to the world, dispensing truth for the public good and for individual happiness.

NOTES

1. Russell M. Nelson, "Drama on the European Stage," *Ensign* 21 (December 1991): 15; emphasis in original.

2. April 26, 1996.

3. Joseph Smith Jr., *History of The Church of Jesus Christ of Latter-day Saints,* ed. B. H. Roberts, 2d ed., rev., 7 vols. (Salt Lake City: Deseret Book, 1971), 4:269.

4. Brigham Young, in *Journal of Discourses,* 26 vols. (Liverpool: F. D. Richards, 1855–86), 10:290, 15 May 1864.

5. Brigham Young, in *Journal of Discourses,* 12:257, 9 August 1868.

6. Arthur Henry King, "The Idea of a Mormon University," *BYU Studies* 13, no. 2 (winter 1973): 115.

7. See King, "The Idea of a Mormon University," 117.

8. See King, "The Idea of a Mormon University," 117.

9. See King, "The Idea of a Mormon University," 117–18.

10. James W. Cannon, "Mathematical Parables," *BYU Studies* 34, no. 4 (1994–95): 94.

11. "The Family: A Proclamation to the World," *Ensign* 25 (November 1995): 102.

12. See King, "The Idea of a Mormon University," 119; also 2 Nephi 9:28–40 and Moroni 9:18–20.

13. President Dallin H. Oaks stated: "Our reason for *being* is to be a university. But our reason for *being a university* is to encourage and prepare young men and women to rise to their full spiritual potential as sons and daughters of God." Dallin H. Oaks, "Inaugural Response," 12 November 1971, 18, emphasis in original. L. Tom Perry Special Collections, Harold B. Lee Library, Brigham Young University, Provo, Utah.

CHAPTER 2

A Zion University and the Search for Truth

(25 AUGUST 1997)

THE QUEST FOR TRUTH and knowledge is as old as time. From the beginning men and women have searched for truth in the hope of better understanding life's purposes and improving life. The temptation put before Adam and Eve in the Garden of Eden was that of knowledge. If they partook of the forbidden fruit from the "tree of the knowledge of good and evil" (Moses 3:17), they were promised: "Ye shall be as gods, knowing good and evil. And when the woman saw that the tree was good for food . . . and a tree to be desired to make her wise, she . . . did eat" (Moses 4:11–12).

Just as Adam and Eve desired knowledge to become more like God, so Abraham's desire for knowledge was linked to his quest to be a more righteous person. He stated: "I sought for the blessings of the fathers, and the right whereunto I should be ordained to administer the same; having been myself a follower of righteousness, desiring also to be one who possessed great knowledge, and to be a greater follower of righteousness" (Abraham 1:2).

With the same spirit, Aristotle described the importance of possessing knowledge so that one can practice virtue and take those actions that will improve not only one's own life but the lives of others. He said: "In practical matters the end is not mere speculative knowledge of what is to be done, but rather the doing of it. It is not enough to know about Virtue, then, but we must endeavour to possess it, and to use it, or to take any other steps that may make us good."[1]

As Aristotle pointed out, knowledge is not the end but an important means to the end. It provides the basis for understanding, for living, and for becoming. He understood that knowledge for knowledge's sake alone was not fulfilling. Just as Adam, Eve, and Abraham desired knowledge in order to be better people, so Aristotle associated knowledge with goodness. This same principle was taught by the Lord to the Prophet Joseph Smith: "And if a person gains more knowledge and intelligence in this life through his diligence and obedience than another, he will have so much the advantage in the world to come" (D&C 130:19). And further, "It is impossible for a man [or woman] to be saved in ignorance" (D&C 131:6).

God's Omniscience

The Savior's injunction "Be ye therefore perfect, even as your Father which is in heaven is perfect" (Matthew 5:48) sets a standard for us. One of God's principal attributes is that of omniscience. The scriptural record provides assurance that God is infinite in His understanding (see Psalm 147:5), is all-knowing (see

2 Nephi 9:20), and possesses a fullness of truth (see D&C 93:11).
Elder Neal A. Maxwell has written:

> God, who knows the beginning from the end, knows,
> therefore, all that is in between. . . .
>
> Below the scripture that declares that God knows "all
> things" there is no footnote reading "*except* that God is a
> little weak in geophysics"! We do not worship a God who
> simply forecasts a generally greater frequency of earth-
> quakes in the last days before the second coming of His
> Son; He knows precisely when and where all these will
> occur. God has even prophesied that the Mount of Olives
> will cleave in twain at a precise latter-day time as Israel is
> besieged. (Zechariah 14:4.)
>
> There are no qualifiers, only flat and absolute asser-
> tions of the omniscience of God.[2]

The Savior describes omniscience as the glory of God, which
is "intelligence, or . . . light and truth" and then states that "light
and truth forsake that evil one" (D&C 93:36–37). Intelligence is
not only the capacity to analyze, synthesize, and store information
but also the disposition to act righteously.[3] As noted earlier, our
first parents, the prophet Abraham, and Aristotle understood this
important linkage.

John the Baptist bore record that Jesus received a fullness of
truth from the Father. John told the Jews: "God giveth not the
Spirit by measure unto him. The Father loveth the Son, and hath
given all things into his hand" (John 3:34–35). The process by
which we obtain knowledge and gain access to truth is "line upon
line, precept upon precept, here a little and there a little" (2 Nephi
28:30). The Savior also "received not of the fulness at the first"
(D&C 93:12–13), but, given His perfection and Godly status in

premortality, the Spirit was given Him in full measure. He grew from "grace to grace" until He received a fullness of truth and light. Christ described Himself as "the light of the world" (John 8:12), and John called Christ "the true Light, which lighteth every man [and woman] that cometh into the world" (John 1:9). Peter, James, and John became special witnesses of His extraordinary light when they beheld Him in His glory on the mount as the "only begotten of the Father" (John 1:14). The three Apostles reported that Christ's "face did shine as the sun, and his raiment was white as the light" (Matthew 17:2). It is significant that John links the Savior's light and truth with His royal birth (see John 1:4–14). In the appearance of the Father and the Son to the Prophet Joseph Smith, Joseph, too, became a witness of their omniscience, or light and truth. He describes the pillar of light as "above the brightness of the sun" and Their personages as having "brightness and glory" beyond "all description" (Joseph Smith–History 1:16–17).

Man's Search for Truth

Not only are the Father and Son filled with light and, therefore, possessors of all knowledge, wisdom, and understanding, but we are told that it is possible for us to receive light and truth until we are "glorified in truth and [know] all things" (D&C 93:28). The eternal potential of men and women includes a fullness of light and truth.

As noted above, the first principle underlying the acquisition of knowledge and intelligence is diligence (i.e., persistent mental and physical exertion). Generally, the acquisition of knowledge is in proportion to one's effort to learn. As students apply themselves to a particular subject, their capacity to understand increases, and their mastery of the subject allows them to use the discipline to inform others, to produce innovations, and to discover new truths.

The second principle is obedience to law. The discovery of secular truth generally occurs when certain principles are followed. First, a hypothesis is formulated that relates cause and effect. Second, data is gathered, and then the hypothesis is tested. An error term is usually included in the model to represent the unknown variables that have been omitted. The smaller the error term in the test, the greater one's confidence in the results. A large error term will lead one to reject the hypothesis.

The acquisition of sacred knowledge follows the same principles. Spiritual truths are received through faith and obedience. Joseph Smith stated "that when a man works by faith he works by mental exertion instead of physical force."[4] Diligent mental exertion is required in one's desires and efforts to learn sacred truths. The mental exertion required in the laboratory of faith is at least as much as that required in the art studio or the science lab. Further, the principle of diligence in the discovery of spiritual truth is a necessary but not a sufficient condition. Spiritual truth is known only through the Spirit, and obedience to God's commandments is required in order to access the Holy Ghost (see 1 Corinthians 2:9–14).

In this dispensation, revelation has made clear the responsibility of each person to search for truth—both secular and sacred. We are to be "instructed . . . in theory, in principle, in doctrine, in the law of the gospel. . . . Of things both in heaven and in the earth . . . ; things which have been, things which are, things which must shortly come to pass . . . ; the wars and the perplexities of the nations . . . ; and a knowledge also of countries . . . and . . . languages, tongues, and people" (D&C 88:78–79; 90:15).

We are commanded to seek "diligently and teach one another words of wisdom; yea, seek ye out of the best books words of wisdom; seek learning, even by study and also by faith" (D&C 88:118).

Here are some of Brigham Young's comments concerning the purpose of mortality:

"This life is worth as much to us as any life in the eternities of the Gods."[5]

"The object of this existence is to learn, which we can only do a little at a time."[6]

"What are we here for? To learn to enjoy more, and to increase in knowledge and in experience."[7]

"The whole mortal existence of man is neither more nor less than a preparatory state given to finite beings, a space wherein they may improve themselves for a higher state of being."[8]

We have the privilege of being engaged in the loftiest of pursuits at Brigham Young University—the search for truth and the dispensing of it. As individuals we are internally motivated by our divine nature to pursue truth. The core of our being is intelligence, or "light and truth." The scripture states that "man was also in the beginning with God. Intelligence, or the light of truth, was not created or made, neither indeed can be" (D&C 93:29). A part of us has always existed. It is intelligence, or light. We are told that "intelligence cleaveth unto intelligence . . . ; light cleaveth unto light" (D&C 88:40). One light to which our intelligence cleaves is the added light given at birth called the Light of Christ. Every human being receives this light so that he or she may know good from evil and be invited to do good (see Moroni 7:15–16). No wonder people hunger for truth. The insatiable desire is innate within each person and is enhanced by the Savior's light. It is a driving force that propels us along the path of eternal progression.

When we act on the light, more light is received. When we lose light through sin, the insatiable desire may be partially or wholly reduced as our capacity to accept additional light is diminished.

The Search for Truth at Brigham Young University

What is BYU's role among the major universities in the search for truth? The purpose of any university is at least fourfold. The first is to discover truth; the second is to organize those discoveries; the third is to store knowledge for current and future generations; and the fourth is to teach truth to students and others. At this university we add one additional function. Students are to be taught how to live for the eternities. Where is BYU in this process?

From the beginning the university has emphasized teaching, or the dissemination of truth. Brigham Young Academy was a normal school established for the purpose of training teachers. The quality of teaching is still critical. A hallmark of this university is the attention that faculty give to students. I have interviewed a number of BYU graduates who are now graduate students at other universities. I have asked them about their progress relative to their colleagues from other highly reputable institutions. Invariably the students share with me the fears and concerns they had at the time they entered graduate school. At first, like almost every other graduate student, they were unsure regarding their ability to compete. Within three to four months, however, many realized that their BYU education was equal or superior to the undergraduate experience of their friends. When asked about the strengths of their BYU experience, their answers often pointed to the quality of instruction and the close relationships they had with BYU faculty members. Recently an outstanding graduate of one of the top three or four major universities in

America enrolled at BYU for additional undergraduate training. The reason given was that he was unable to obtain the quality of instruction desired because faculty access was almost nonexistent at the other school. At the particular institution in question, emphasis on research seemed to preclude faculty from spending time with undergraduate students outside the classroom.

Given a 90:10 undergraduate-to-graduate ratio and an emphasis on quality instruction, is the search for truth at BYU relegated to a second priority? The answer must be no! The discovery of truth is as important at this university as its dissemination, for a number of reasons. The quest for and discovery of knowledge helps the "(1) . . . faculty to remain current in their disciplines and 'alive' in teaching; (2) scholarly work contributes directly to the education of the students, both graduate and undergraduate; (3) scholarly work establishes the credibility of BYU and the . . . faculty in national academic/professional circles."[9]

The search for truth is part of the divine nature, and I believe there are some secular truths yet to be discovered that have been reserved for the faithful. We must be contributors to the world's storehouse of knowledge to improve the lives of others.

During the past three decades, creativity in the arts and scientific research have become an integral part of BYU's program. I use the word *integral* for a special reason. My experience at five universities suggests that the best teachers, sacred or secular, are engaged in the discovery process. The discovery of truth and the creation of beauty are exhausting experiences, but they are also exhilarating ones as new light and energy are unleashed. Key attributes of a good teacher are knowledge and enthusiasm. Both are enhanced by the discovery process.

If Brigham Young University is to be a Zion university, as described by Presidents John Taylor and Spencer W. Kimball, the search for truth must be an integral part of the BYU experience. President Taylor said: "You will see the day that Zion will be as far ahead of the outside world in everything pertaining to learning of every kind as we are to-day in regard to religious matters."[10]

President Spencer W. Kimball spoke extensively on this subject on a number of occasions. Typical is the following:

> This university shares with other universities the hope and the labor involved in rolling back the frontiers of knowledge, but we also know that, through divine revelation, there are yet "many great and important things" (Articles of Faith 1:9) to be given to mankind which will have an intellectual and spiritual impact far beyond what mere men can imagine. Thus, at this university among faculty, students, and administration, there is, and there must be, an excitement and an expectation about the very nature and future of knowledge. That underlies the uniqueness of BYU.[11]

The learning process requires diligent mental exertion in both secular and spiritual dimensions, which then must be combined with obedience to secular and spiritual laws. These actions will guarantee access to the Spirit, which will accelerate the discovery process.

It is obvious from the above statements that a Zion university is not a copy of other institutions. The paradigm is faithful scholars involved in extending the frontiers of knowledge while engaging their students in the discovery process. In the words of President Kimball: "This university is not of the world any more than the Church is of the world, and it must not be made over in the image of the world."[12]

Each member of the faculty, staff, and administration must be filled with truth. We must be not only the best scholars, the best staff and administrators, but also the best people we can be. This is crucial in light of the unique institution of which we are a part and its connection with the Church.

Academic Freedom and the Search for Truth

In the search for truth, the university has a responsibility to provide an environment in which the discovery of truth is fostered. Two environmental conditions are essential for the discovery process to be as fruitful as possible. The first is freedom of belief or freedom of thought. If anyone understands the importance of the right to pursue one's own beliefs, it is the LDS people. As stated in the Statement on Academic Freedom (SAF) at Brigham Young University:

> Individual freedom lies at the core of both religious and academic life. Freedom of thought, belief, inquiry, and expression are crucial no less to the sacred than to the secular quest for truth. Historically, in fact, freedom of conscience and freedom of intellect form a common root, from which grow both religious and academic freedom.[13]

The right to ask difficult questions, to rigorously analyze results, and to report one's work are vital to the discovery and dissemination process. We believe that faculty members should be able to research and teach in their disciplines without interference as long as a second environmental condition is allowed to operate. Before proceeding to that condition, it should be noted that individual academic freedom is "broad" and "presumptive," whereas any limitations coming from the second condition are "exceptional and limited."[14]

The second environmental condition concerns the right of an academic institution to pursue its defined mission and to be free from outside control. Every university (public, private, religious, or nonreligious) places limitations on individual freedom in order to create an environment that fosters the discovery and dissemination of truth within the context of its institutional mission.[15] Public universities, for example, prohibit faculty members from advocating religious beliefs in class in order to preserve a separation between church and state. Most universities limit faculty members in denigrating individuals or groups based on race, gender, religion, or nationality. Some universities establish obscenity standards that prohibit the use of certain language, films, and written materials in the classroom.

From the beginning Brigham Young University has been open in declaring its mission and expectations while at the same time protecting the freedom of the individual as much as possible. The statement made by Brigham Young to Karl G. Maeser regarding the responsibility to teach by the Spirit encompasses the two expectations enunciated in the university's Statement on Academic Freedom.[16] The first expectation is that all LDS members of the university community should "live lives of loyalty to the restored gospel."[17] For LDS members of the faculty, staff, and administration, this expectation has been defined as accepting "as a condition of employment the standards of conduct consistent with qualifying for temple privileges."[18] For people of other faiths, the standard is the Honor Code coupled with a willingness to "respect the LDS nature of the university and its mission, while the university in turn respects their religious convictions."[19]

The second expectation is a clarification of the first. It asks community members not to engage in "behavior or expression [that] *seriously and adversely affects* the university mission or the

Church."[20] Examples include public behavior or expression that "contradicts or opposes, rather than analyzes or discusses, fundamental Church doctrine or policy" or that "deliberately attacks or derides the Church or its general leaders."[21] In addition, BYU's Statement on Academic Freedom contains an important safeguard. It states: "A faculty member shall not be found in violation of the academic freedom standards unless the faculty member can fairly be considered aware that the expression violates the standards."[22]

Why are these expectations important to the university's mission? Do they relate to the discovery and dissemination of truth? When one understands our faith, one realizes that the university's expectations are, in fact, encased in the enabling principle of obedience. Obedience to sacred laws is necessary for access to the Spirit. Our faith teaches and our experience confirms that the Holy Spirit is an important aid in the discovery and dissemination of truth—sacred or secular. The university's mission could not be accomplished and community members would be handicapped in the search for truth if the condition of faithfulness were to be eliminated. This condition supports more than the establishment of a congenial community of believers engaged in higher education. For us, the condition is fundamental to the educational process.

Some have stated that the principle of obedience is inconsistent with the principle of agency. Elder Neal A. Maxwell has commented on this point as follows:

> We are in a universe of physical and spiritual laws; it is these which demand obedience. It is actually enlightened obedience to follow freely those laws which produce the desired result. . . . That course is hardly blind obedience. . . .

> Freedom does not always multiply options. A scientist wishing to create water must use two parts hydrogen and one part oxygen. "There is a law. . . ."
>
> Freedom does not free us from law.[23]

As declared in BYU's Statement on Academic Freedom, the university mission is to "nourish a community of believing scholars, where students and teachers, guided by the gospel, freely join together to seek truth in charity and virtue. For those who embrace the gospel, BYU offers a far richer and more complete kind of academic freedom than is possible in secular universities because to seek knowledge in the light of revealed truth is, for believers, to be free indeed."[24]

Recent Challenges to BYU's Statement on Academic Freedom

In recent years, a number of organizations representing institutions of higher education have openly criticized universities that combine the sacred and the secular. Their main argument is that in such institutions, academic freedom is diminished.

Part of the reason for misstatements made about BYU is that many people are opposed to BYU's mission and have an agenda to undermine it. Professor Douglas Laycock, the Alice McKean Young Regents Chair in Law and associate dean for research at the University of Texas Law School, has commented on the absolutist position of the secularists in higher education as follows:

> The secular side controls 97% or so of the institutions. Can the three percent have some existence of their own? Can the three percent strike their own balance of religious and academic commitments? Or is the secular

model so absolutist that it cannot tolerate a three percent minority with a different solution? That is the issue.[25]

Professor Laycock has carefully analyzed BYU's Statement on Academic Freedom in light of AAUP guidelines and has made the following statement:

> Ironically, by purporting to expel from the academic community any school that invokes the limitations clause, or to deprive schools of any benefit even when they invoke it, the AAUP ensures that few academically serious universities will ever disclose potential limits on academic freedom. The most notable exception is Brigham Young, which has recently completed a courageous effort to state as carefully as possible the limitations on academic freedom necessary to its mission.[26]

Laycock further states: "The Brigham Young Statement is probably as full a disclosure as can reasonably be achieved."[27]

Although it is important that outside scholars consider the Brigham Young University Statement on Academic Freedom to be fair and evenhanded, it is far more important that our university community understand that our statement, which was generated by a faculty committee drawn from disciplines across campus, is a fair, open, and clear expression of university values. The genius of our statement is that it gives faculty members clear notice of conduct or expression that may be considered to be in violation of the statement. "A faculty member shall not be found in violation of the academic freedom standards unless the faculty member can *fairly* be considered aware that the expression violates the standards."[28]

Any criticism that charges the university with creating an

unclear standard quite simply misses the mark. The university mission and the expectations necessary to preserve and further that mission are clear.

Summary

Brigham Young University is a wonderful place filled with extraordinary people acquiring light and truth. The mission of the university was defined one hundred twenty years ago by a prophet of God. There has been no deviation since, nor will there be. We must be diligent in our efforts to safeguard individual academic freedom while fostering the university's unique purpose. Faithful faculty and staff understand that all truth is spiritual. They know by experience that the search for sacred and secular truth is enhanced by a spiritual environment that provides additional light. Ultimately there is no dichotomy. Truth is truth! The search for truth at Brigham Young University will prosper over time because of the way the community lives and the peace that prevails.

Also, the discovery process will become an even more integral part of the instruction that is offered as original scholarship increasingly informs outstanding teachers. If the common bond of the gospel stretches across the campus and includes every discipline—and if we are diligent in obeying both sacred and secular laws—we will have the respect of the One who counts. In the end, scholars and prophets will measure us by what we produce.

NOTES

1. Aristotle, *Nicomachean Ethics,* X, 9, 1.
2. Neal A. Maxwell, *All These Things Shall Give Thee Experience* (Salt Lake City: Deseret Book, 1980), 7; emphasis in original.

3. See David H. Yarn Jr., "My Age of Preparation," *BYU 1995–96 Speeches* (Provo, Utah: Brigham Young University, 1996), 315–21.

4. N. B. Lundwall, comp., *Lectures on Faith* (Salt Lake City: Bookcraft, n.d.), 61 [7:3].

5. Brigham Young, in *Journal of Discourses,* 26 vols. (Liverpool: F. D. Richards, 1855–86), 9:170, 26 January 1862.

6. Brigham Young, in *Journal of Discourses,* 9:167, 26 January 1862.

7. Brigham Young, in *Journal of Discourses,* 14:228, 16 September 1871.

8. Brigham Young, in *Journal of Discourses,* 1:334, 5 December 1853.

9. "A Model for Directing Scholarly Work at Brigham Young University," (Brigham Young University, Office of Research and Creative Activities, 1994), 6.

10. John Taylor, in *Journal of Discourses,* 21:100, 13 April 1879.

11. Spencer W. Kimball, "Installation of and Charge to the President," in *Educating Zion,* eds. John W. Welch and Don E. Norton (Provo, Utah: BYU Studies, 1996), 76.

12. Spencer W. Kimball, "Second Century Address," in *Educating Zion,* 66.

13. Statement on Academic Freedom at Brigham Young University (SAF), BYU 1997–98 Undergraduate Catalog, xvii.

14. SAF, xix.

15. See "Editor's Preface," George S. Worgul, Jr., *Issues in Academic Freedom* (Pittsburgh, Pa.: Duquesne University Press, 1992), viii–ix.

16. Karl G. Maeser, "History of the Academy," in *Educating Zion,* 2.

17. Faculty Rank and Status: Professorial Policy, Policy and Procedures Section, University Electronic Handbook (rev. 1 September 1994), sec. 3.1.1.

18. Administrative/Staff Employment Policy, University Electronic Handbook (rev. 4 August 1997); see also Faculty Rank and Status: Professorial Policy, sec. 3.1.1.

19. SAF, xviii.

20. SAF, xix; emphasis in original.

21. SAF, xix.

22. SAF, xix.

23. Neal A. Maxwell, *Deposition of a Disciple* (Salt Lake City: Deseret Book, 1976), 96–97.

24. SAF, xx.

25. Douglas Laycock, "The Rights of Religious Academic Communities," *Journal of College and University Law* 20, no. 1 (summer 1993): 26.

26. Laycock, " The Rights of Religious Academic Communities," 29.

27. Laycock, " The Rights of Religious Academic Communities," 32.

28. SAF, xix; emphasis added.

CHAPTER 3

Children of the Covenant

(8 SEPTEMBER 1998)

At THE BEGINNING of each school year, we are excited to meet the freshman and transfer students and feel their energy and enthusiasm. Conversations with parents of new students reveal a deep appreciation for Brigham Young University and its mission. As the world drifts farther away from well-proven principles, parents are concerned for the moral and spiritual welfare of their young people as they leave home for college life. An e-mail message received from the father of a new freshman is typical of parents' feelings. The message reads:

> Dear President Bateman,
>
> Thank[s] for taking the time to speak with us new-student parents last Thursday afternoon. [The parent meeting] and the "commencement" later that night were a . . . highlight in our trip to bring our daughter to school. I was especially impressed by two things:
>
> [The] sincere effort to get the freshmen involved;

[The] down-to-earth manner in discussing the challenges students will face.

The father then concluded his message with the following statement:

> I felt something in those meetings that I haven't felt for a long time; the excitement of being a part of a community that is really doing something important, meaningful, and beneficial to the world. We know our daughter is in good hands and are thrilled that she's able to attend BYU.
>
> Best regards . . . [1]

The theme for my remarks centers on the father's feelings of "being part of a community that is . . . doing something important." There are two parts to the statement. I wish to discuss both and then suggest ways in which each member of the community can live up to the opportunities that are here.

The father indicated that he felt the "excitement of being part of [the Brigham Young University] community." What is the BYU community? What is the source of excitement felt by the father? Is BYU making a meaningful contribution to the world? I believe that BYU's mission is among the most important on earth! What is it? I wish to address these questions in the hope that our view of the university will be broadened and our commitment deepened.

The Mission of Brigham Young University

I would like to relate an incident that took place in 1885, ten years after the founding of Brigham Young Academy. In those days the school was funded by local donations with little support from Church headquarters, and the college had fallen on hard times. There was not enough money to pay teachers or provide supplies. The situation was desperate, and it appeared that the academy's doors would close. Zina Young Williams, dean of women and a daughter of Brigham Young, initiated a meeting with President John Taylor in the hope of obtaining Church help. The story unfolds as follows:

After listening to Sister Williams's plea for help, President Taylor took her hand "in a fatherly way" and said:

> My dear child, I have something of importance to tell you that I know will make you happy. I have been visited by your father. He came to me in the silence of the night clothed in brightness and with a face beaming with love and confidence told me things of great importance and among others that the school being taught by Brother [Karl G.] Maeser was accepted in the heavens and was a part of the great plan of life and salvation; . . . and there was a bright future in store for . . . preparing . . . the children of the covenant for future usefulness in the Kingdom of God, and that Christ himself was directing, and had a care over this school.[2]

In spite of the dark hour overshadowing the academy in 1885, one can say with hindsight that it did have a "bright future." As one compares today's marvelous campus nestled against the Wasatch Mountains with those early beginnings in downtown Provo, the connection is almost unrecognizable in physical terms. The small seedling Zina Young Williams tried to protect has developed into a mature forest. There is a stark contrast between the few dozen students gathered from local communities in 1885 and today's almost 30,000 students assembled from all 50 states and 117 foreign countries. But elaborate facilities and a large student body are not sufficient to fulfill President Taylor's dream. Brigham Young's statement to President John Taylor is fulfilled only if the university prepares "children of the covenant for future usefulness in the Kingdom of God." The mission of BYU encompasses the academic but is more—much more. Who are the "children of the covenant," and how does the university prepare them to be useful in the kingdom and the world?

The Children of the Covenant

The BYU community is composed of children of the covenant. In order to know who these people are, one must know something about the covenant. The revealed gospel of Jesus Christ is called the "new and everlasting covenant." We believe that it embraces every set of promises that God has made or will make with men and women on this earth (see D&C 132:5–7, 133:57). One enters into this covenant through faith, repentance, and baptism. One continues in the covenant through obedience to gospel principles and by participation in even higher covenants.

The "new and everlasting covenant" is the most potent force shaping the destiny of Brigham Young University. It produces the light that helps us see the university's mission. It generates the power that draws us together and focuses our energy in the discovery of knowledge. The bond that creates the special BYU community is not just the contractual relationship each person has with the university but the covenantal relationship that exists between us and the Lord. Members of the Church have covenanted at baptism and in the temple to live a righteous life and to contribute to the building of the kingdom. The university is part of the kingdom.

A large portion of the faculty, staff, and students are members of The Church of Jesus Christ of Latter-day Saints. As such, they have entered into covenants with the Lord through Church ordinances. What about non-LDS members of the BYU community? They have not participated in these ordinances. Are they covenant makers or is their relationship only contractual? It is my view that nonmember faculty, staff, and students may enjoy more than a contractual relationship with the university. It is my belief that non-LDS faculty and students become covenant participants when they agree to support the university's mission and participate with full heart to preserve the covenantal environment. I arrived at this conclusion after reflecting on many conversations with nonmember faculty and after reading a letter written by a new member of our faculty who is non-LDS. The letter was written by him to former colleagues explaining why he left his position at their university to join us. With his permission, I share a portion of the letter:

> For those of you who are unfamiliar with BYU, it is the flagship university of The Church of Jesus Christ of Latter-day Saints. . . . Neither [my wife] nor I are members of the LDS Church, but as embodied in its university and the warmth of its members' acceptance of us, we have found it to represent a remarkable testament to God's work on earth. Indeed, Brigham Young University is one of the rare remaining examples of what all religiously affiliated universities once aspired to be—an institution that sees its students as persons of infinite worth and believes that their education for faithful lives represents the world's

best hope for a humane and productive future. The educational program and student experience at BYU [are] built around such core values.[3]

The letter's message closely parallels Brigham Young's statement to John Taylor. The letter illustrates the faculty member's understanding of and willingness to contribute to the university's mission. He is committed to prepare students for "faithful lives" in the hope of building a better world. He understands that each person is of infinite worth and is prepared to treat them as such. He is committed to working in a covenant environment. His heart and mind indicate that his relationship is more than a contractual one.

Conversations with other non-LDS faculty at BYU have revealed the same commitment and attitude. Almost all see students in an infinite light. We are grateful that non-LDS faculty assembled at BYU are true to the university's purpose and that our standards are your standards. We express appreciation for the contributions you make and want you to know that you would be as comfortable in the temple with us as you are in the classroom.

All of us, members and nonmembers, are affected by the covenantal environment that exists. The infinite and eternal relationship is the engine that empowers us to change lives intellectually and spiritually. President Gordon B. Hinckley has described the unique features of BYU. With regard to the faculty, he stated that they "feel as much at home in the house of the Lord as they feel in the classrooms of this university. When all is said and done, it is not this elaborate campus that really counts. It is the faculty who teach you, who lead you, who encourage you, who help you find your way as you go forward with your studies. This . . . is an element of the singular BYU experience."[4]

Although I have suggested that all members of BYU are children of the covenant, President Young's reference was directly applicable to students. His concern was with you, the student body. The "bright future" that lay in store for the university is now your present. The purpose of the university is to help you become useful in the kingdom of God. The Lord's definition of intelligence encompasses both intellectual and spiritual acumen (see D&C 93:36–37). He is concerned with you as a whole person. That is why Brigham Young wanted the students to experience every subject taught under the influence of the Spirit.

There are data that confirm the status of BYU students as "children of the covenant." You are different in many respects from students at other universities. In a recent survey of 311 colleges by *The Princeton Review,* BYU students ranked first on the "stone-cold sober" list. Just as important, you also ranked first for "students [who] pray on a regular basis." You helped BYU rank second in the "town-gown relations" category.[5] This is important. BYU is a significant part of the Provo-Orem community. We must be good citizens.

There is another survey in which BYU students participate that highlights some other characteristics. It is called the "College Student Experiences Questionnaire," in which thirty major universities participate. Participants include students from Duke, Pennsylvania State, UCLA, Washington State, Southern Methodist, and others. The survey is a nationally normed, stratified, random sample of 25,000 students with 1,500 BYU participants. The survey has been administered over the years, with the last survey taken in March 1997. Some interesting comparisons between BYU students and their counterparts are the following:

• BYU students spend significantly more hours per week doing school work.

• BYU students spend significantly more hours per week working at a job.

• BYU students are much less likely to have their expenses paid by their family.

• The parents of BYU students are more educated than their counterparts.

• BYU students are more likely to engage in activities relating to art, music, and the theater.

• BYU students experience a significantly higher number of writing experiences in the form of essay exams, term papers, and written reports.

The questionnaire also revealed that BYU students are above average in gaining a broad general education, in acquiring knowledge and skills for work, and in developing their own values and ethical standards. The data are highly complimentary of this student body. Research has shown that the most important factor in student learning is the quality of effort students themselves apply to their institution's available resources. It is clear that our students are more mature and more committed as they devote additional time and energy to both study and work. These characteristics suggest that you take seriously your responsibilities as "children of the covenant."

An international diplomat visiting campus asked two questions that reflect on us as a covenant people. He had spent the morning lecturing and visiting with students and faculty. He then came to my office for a brief exchange. The first question he asked was, "Are all the buildings new?" When told that some were fifty to sixty years old, he replied, "But they are so clean." The second question asked was, "Why is everyone so happy?" Because he knew little about us, my answer centered on our beliefs and our standards of behavior. The short answer, had he known more about us, could have been, "Because we are a covenant people!"

I arrived at the university in January 1996, believing that Brigham Young University was "in the process of becoming a 'Zion university.'"[6] It was my belief then that considerable progress had been made over the years in achieving the goal of academic excellence in a climate of faith but that there was still a long road to travel before the designation "a Zion university" would be appropriate.

In contrast to my views of three years ago, the recent impression was that Brigham Young University *is* a Zion university. At first I resisted the notion. None of us believes that we have reached our potential—either as scholars or as Saints. On the other hand, perhaps Tessa Meyer Santiago was right when she implied that Zion is not a destination but a covenant people with "a knowledge of the gospel and the resurrected Christ in [their] hearts," all journeying to the promised land.[7]

No wonder the father of the young freshman daughter felt the excitement and sensed the importance of this university. He felt the influence of the Lord's Spirit as all of us are committed to preparing the children of the covenant for useful lives in God's kingdom.

The Challenge

I close with a challenge for all of us to be true to the promises we have made—both to the university and to the Lord. Obedience to true principles is not a burden when one's relationship to God is understood and when one has a burning within regarding the verity of the restored gospel.

NOTES

1. Personal letter in my possession.

2. Leonard J. Arrington, ed., *The Presidents of the Church* (Salt Lake City: Deseret Book, 1986), 1089.

3. Professor Tom Morgan to George Washington University law faculty, 12 January 1998, copy of letter in my possession.

4. Gordon B. Hinckley, "The BYU Experience," *BYU 1997–1998 Speeches* (Provo, Utah: Brigham Young University, 1998), 63.

5. See *The Best 311 Colleges—1999 Edition* (New York: Random House, 1998).

6. Merrill J. Bateman, "A Zion University," *BYU Speeches 1995–1996* (Provo, Utah: Brigham Young University, 1998), 125.

7. Tessa Meyer Santiago, "Under Covenant toward the Promised Land: Section 136 as a Latter-day Type," *BYU 1996–97 Speeches* (Provo, Utah: Brigham Young University, 1997), 241.

CHAPTER 4

From Pioneer Roots to a World-Class, Worldwide Institution

(23 AUGUST 1999)

IN JUST A FEW months all of us will experience a first that is rare in the history of humankind. We will enter a new millennium. As we approach the end of the 20th century, the torch of enlightenment shines brighter than ever. The opportunity to learn of intellectual and spiritual truths has never been greater. It is now possible for the world's population to read about the latest scientific discovery within hours of the event. It is possible for Church members anywhere in the world to access President Gordon B. Hinckley's latest sermon within minutes of its delivery. The rate of discovery in the world of science is unparalleled. A larger and larger proportion of the world's population recognizes the value of and seeks after higher education. In this milieu, Brigham Young University has begun to flower as a world-class institution with a potential worldwide influence.

As we approach a new millennium, it seems appropriate to pause for a moment and reflect on the university's past, to review some key events that have influenced BYU's journey, and to remember a few of the many wonderful men and women who pioneered our path to excellence. Following the history, I wish to speak of the present in light of four institutional objectives. These objectives are not new, as they are implied by BYU's Mission Statement and the aims documents. In a succinct manner, however, they state the university's reasons for being and the aspirations that guide us. Finally, I will present a brief perspective on the future by looking "through a glass, darkly." Like Paul of old, we only see and "know in part" (1 Corinthians 13:12).

The Past

Most people associated with Brigham Young University are acquainted with its beginnings. At least we are familiar with President Brigham Young's charge to Karl G. Maeser: "You ought not to teach even the alphabet or the multiplication tables without the Spirit of God."[1] We are also familiar with the stories that describe the financial difficulties experienced during the early years. As I reviewed BYU's history, it was apparent that every president of this institution up to President Ernest L. Wilkinson faced the threat of closure. Why? Because there was no money! The university did not have any! The Church had very little! The people had none!

The school was established in a desert by an immigrant people who were in the early stages of forming an economic base. By 1875 economic transactions were still largely founded on barter. There was little money available and even less in circulation. People were paid in-kind with home produce—sometimes from the land and sometimes from the spinning wheel. In spite of the hardships, the LDS people were hungry for education. They prized knowledge, both secular and spiritual. They were willing to sacrifice in order for their children to receive schooling. In this environment, Brigham Young University had its beginnings.

In reviewing the history and progress of the university, I have divided the 125 years into four periods. The first is 1875 to 1900. I have labeled this period "Early Days, Difficult Times." The second covers a 50-year period from 1900 to 1950. These years are a time of transition from a small normal school to a major university. The label I have affixed is "Building a University Foundation." The third time frame is coincident with the tenure of President Ernest L. Wilkinson, 1951 to 1971. That twenty-year period is one of astounding growth. I have called the Wilkinson era "Growth and Laying a Foundation of Excellence." The final period covers the last twenty-eight years, 1971–1999. Caps on the size of the university allowed its constituents to focus on quality rather than quantity. Improvements in almost every facet of university life occurred, from the classroom to the lab, from the library to the research productivity of the faculty. The title for the last period is "A Time of Excellence."

I do not intend to review the university's history. A full review would be lengthy and laborious. Rather, I will describe one or two key events and, in some cases, relate a story illustrating the legacy inherited from those who have gone before. Perhaps by reviewing our pioneer beginnings and reliving a few key events, we will have a clearer view of what the future may hold. Most important, doing so will help us renew our resolve to continue building an institution of manifest destiny. As I have reviewed various documents relating to the past, it has been interesting to note that every time a crisis occurred that threatened the existence of BYU, the heavens were opened and assurance was given regarding the future of Brigham Young University. We now turn to its fragile beginnings.

1875–1900: Early Days, Difficult Times

There is reason to believe that President Brigham Young had been thinking of establishing a system of LDS educational institutions to serve the population of Utah at least two years before the founding of Brigham Young Academy. At a minimum, there is clear evidence that he wished to form a high-quality university that would include the teaching of religious principles at its core. The basis for this conclusion is a letter written in 1873 by Colonel Thomas L. Kane to President Young that contains the first known reference to a school called Brigham Young University. Colonel Kane's letter stated:

> I know your sentiments; that Utah should before this [1873] have been educating her own teachers, and preparing if not publishing her own text books. The young fledglings who would resort to our Eastern seminaries of learning—to learn what you will hardly be able to unteach them all their days—should even now be training in the Brigham Young University, normal college of the highest grade, to officiate as "Zion" tutors and professors.[2]

In an earlier communication, President Young had told Colonel Kane of his desire to found an educational institution to serve as an offset to the "modern unfaith."[3]

In addition to Colonel Kane's letter, a newspaper account of a meeting between Warren Dusenberry and President Young indicated the same. Warren Dusenberry and his brother had established a school in Provo in 1869. By 1875 the school was about to be closed for financial reasons. Upon learning of its pending closure, President Young asked Warren Dusenberry to visit with him. Dusenberry reported the following:

I received a communication from Pres. Brigham Young to call upon him. I did so. After expressing his disapproval of our breaking up the school . . . he said he intended endowing an institution of learning with sufficient means to make it an honor to the Territory and her people. . . . He requested me, in company with others, to immediately draft the necessary papers for founding the BYA. I knew it would require a great struggle, yet I knew it would be what it is today.[4]

President Young then singled out six prominent men and one woman to serve as trustees. Abraham O. Smoot was elected president of the board. President Young stipulated that the "Old and New Testaments, the Book of Mormon and the Book of Doctrine and Covenants shall be read and their doctrines inculcated in the Academy" as a counter to the trend of the day that was to eliminate religion from higher education.[5]

Karl G. Maeser was principal of the Twentieth Ward School in Salt Lake City at the time Brigham Young Academy was founded. Shortly thereafter, his schoolhouse was severely damaged by an explosion at a nearby arsenal. Maeser sought out the bishop to report the damage and found him with President Young. Upon learning that Brother Maeser no longer had a building to meet in, Brigham immediately called him to serve as the principal of the new school in Provo. The new school opened in January 1876 under the temporary leadership of Warren Dusenberry. Brother Maeser arrived in April 1876.

Two years later, shortly after the death of Brigham Young, Karl Maeser had a dream. In the dream he was given the design of a new building, but he did not know its purpose. At the time they were meeting in Lewis Hall on Center Street and Third West. In

1884, six years after the dream, Lewis Hall burned to the ground, leaving the school without a place to meet. As the Lewis building was burning, Karl Maeser understood the meaning of his dream six years earlier. His description of the dream is as follows:

> I found myself entering a spacious hallway with open doors leading into many rooms, and saw President Brigham Young and a stranger, while ascending the stairs, beckoning me to follow them. Thus they led me into the upper story containing similar rooms and a large assembly hall, where I lost sight of my guides, and awoke. Deeply impressed with this dream, I drew up the plan of the location shown to me and stowed it away without any apparent purpose for its keeping nor any definite interpretation of its meaning, and it lay there almost forgotten for more than six years, when in January, 1884, the old Academy building was destroyed by fire. The want of new localities caused by that calamity brought into remembrance that paper, which on being submitted suggestively to the board, was at once approved of, and our architect, a son of President Young, instructed to put into proper . . . shape. . . . When in future days people will ask for the name of the wise designer of the interior of this edifice, let the answer be: Brigham Young.[6]

The new building that was completed in 1892 is known today as the Academy or Education Building on what was the lower campus. Given the subsequent history of the building and Brother Maeser's story that Brigham Young designed it, one appreciates even more the group of Provo citizens that have banded together to save it.

Brigham Young Academy experienced one financial crisis after another following the Lewis building fire. By the mid-1880s, the school was in dire straits. The faculty and staff received only one-third of their salaries in 1885.[7]

Karl Maeser stayed for another six or seven years until the new building was completed. He was the intellectual and spiritual architect who laid the foundation for today's magnificent institution. George Brimhall, a student of both Dusenberry and Maeser, described the impact that Karl Maeser had on him in the following words: "Judge Dusenberry showed me the road to higher education, but Karl G. Maeser showed me the way to a higher life."[8]

Just as Brother Maeser was the spiritual and intellectual force in the early days of the academy, so Abraham O. Smoot was the financial savior. He was a highly successful businessman, president of the Utah Stake, and mayor of Provo. He died penniless and heavily in debt for personally endorsing loans to save Brigham Young Academy. It is recorded that "his iron will [and administrative abilities] saved the institution a number of times."[9]

Benjamin Cluff Jr. replaced Principal Maeser and served from 1892 to 1903. He proved to be a competent administrator who was quite different in personality and temperament from Karl G. Maeser. At the time of his leaving, Maeser was sixty-three years of age, "staid in appearance, an adherent of Prussian methodology in education, and conservative as well as sober in his demeanor; while Cluff, on the other hand, was only thirty-four, vibrant, impetuous, and imbued with new educational ideas" he had brought from the University of Michigan. "Maeser advocated a closed educational society for the Church, while Cluff gloried in his . . . association with . . . gentile faculty."[10]

President Cluff adroitly resisted the notion that Brigham Young Academy become a feeder school to the University of Utah. He guided the institution through the financial panic of 1893–94 and finally convinced Church leaders to incorporate the academy inside the Church. From 1896 onward, the financial well-being of BYU has been intimately tied to the financial conditions of the Church. Throughout this century [the 20th], sacred funds have provided the means to support the growth and improvements that we now enjoy.

1900–1950: Building a University Foundation

In 1903 the name of the institution was changed to Brigham Young University. The first half of the 20th century was one of dynamic growth as the student body increased from 50 college students to 5,000 by midcentury. The Church assumed all of BYU's past debts in 1918, and a close alliance developed between the Church and the school. During the first decade the normal training school was expanded to include the training of high school teachers.[11] In 1907 the Maeser Memorial Building project was undertaken on Temple Hill—the first building on the upper campus. The faculty sacrificed up to one-half of a year's salary to make it a reality.[12] Five new colleges plus the graduate school were added in the 1920s. The colleges included Education, Arts and Sciences, Commerce and Business Administration, Applied Science, and Fine Arts. Key personnel attracted to the university during this period include Harvey Fletcher, Carl Eyring, Sidney Sperry, Gerrit de Jong, Thomas Martin, Hugh Nibley, Reed Bradford, Clinton Larson, Alma Burton, Herald R. and Harold Glen Clark, and many others.

Jesse Knight and Franklin Harris played major roles in keeping the university moving forward during the first half-century. Jesse Knight, the son of Newel Knight, who was a close friend of the Prophet Joseph Smith, never knew his father, who died at

Winter Quarters after leading the first fifty Saints out of Nauvoo. His mother and eight children made their way to Utah and eventually settled in Utah County for a time. Jesse eventually struck it rich in the mining industry. Through a healing of a daughter and the encouragement of a son, he became a major benefactor of BYU, sustaining it financially over a number of years.

Franklin S. Harris was the fourth leader of the university. He was a major driving force from 1921 to 1944. He attracted strong faculty, built the first library and academic buildings on upper campus, and was an extraordinary defender. He was the first president to travel on official business outside the United States, as he was invited on three separate occasions to present a paper in Japan, help settle 60,000 Jews in Russia, and reorganize the Department of Agriculture for the government of Iran. On the trip to Japan, he invited and then received the first foreign students outside North America to attend the university.[13]

Student enrollments increased significantly in the 1920s and the late 1940s following the two world wars. A hiatus was reached during the Great Depression as Church and university finances came under considerable pressure. Throughout the fifty-year period, Church officials debated the wisdom of maintaining a system of higher education that included a number of junior colleges plus BYU. On numerous occasions declarations were made indicating that the schools would be closed or turned over to the state governments. Eventually, all of the units were transferred with the exception of BYU and Ricks College.

One incident that reveals again the destiny of Brigham Young University occurred during the depths of the Depression. The Church was deeply in debt, and President Heber J. Grant made a trip to New York to meet with the banking community, seeking a substantial loan. One of the conditions levied on the Church by the bankers was the shedding of the educational institutions. Following the meeting with the bankers, President Grant called Church leaders in Salt Lake City to inform them of the outcome. Word quickly spread to Provo that BYU would be closed. University archives contain a document that records an interview with Sidney B. Sperry, who had joined the faculty a year or two before the event. The interview recorded the following:

> Brother Sperry stated that during the early nineteen thirties the depression became so severe that the Church found it impossible to provide financial support for its many enterprises and that when President Grant went to New York to secure a substantial loan it was necessary for him to agree to give up the various colleges which the Church was supporting, including . . . BYU. Brother Sperry said the announcement made him heartsick because so many people had sacrificed so much to keep the Church colleges going, especially . . . BYU.

> Shortly after President Grant made his announcement from New York, Brother Sperry said he awakened in the middle of the night and saw a vision of the Brigham Young University of the future. He saw beautiful modern buildings extending along the entire east bench and saw great concourses of people coming to the University to receive guidance and instruction. In connection with the University he saw a temple and therefore knew that . . . BYU was going to remain a Church institution.

> The following morning Brother Sperry said he advised a number of his colleagues that he was certain the Church was not going to give up BYU. When President Grant returned from New York he said all of the Church junior

colleges would be turned over to the State but that the Church would continue to operate the Brigham Young University.[14]

A sequel to the story occurred almost forty years later when Church leaders were considering two sites for the Provo Temple. One was in front of Y Mountain and the other was in the mouth of Rock Creek Canyon. Before the choice was made, Brother Sperry in a conversation with Cleon Skousen told him that the temple would not be in front of the Y because in his 1930s vision it was further north.[15]

Following World War II, the university suddenly burgeoned. Can you imagine the challenges faced by President Howard S. McDonald and the faculty and staff when the enrollment increased from 1,500 students in the spring of 1945 to 2,700 in the fall of the same year? In today's terms, the increase is equivalent to leaving school last April with 30,000 students and returning this month to find 54,000. It would be another four years before an additional building was added to campus.

1951–1971: Growth and Laying a Foundation of Excellence

The modern era for Brigham Young University began during the 1950s. Although I am not familiar with Church finances during the 1950s, the economic boom that followed World War II must have contributed to the well-being of the Church. Tithing contributions in the 1950s and 1960s would still have been modest, compared with today's figures, if for no other reason than the difference in Church membership. Nevertheless, it is safe to say that the entire second half of the 20th century has been a time of prosperity for the United States and most nations across the earth. It has been an extraordinary time for building the Church and a major university. And that is precisely what happened.

As almost all know, President Ernest L. Wilkinson was a key figure in providing the buildings that Sidney Sperry saw in his dream. The Eyring Science Center was dedicated a short time before President Wilkinson arrived. It was the fifth building on the upper campus. Today there are about three hundred buildings. A large proportion of upper campus was built during the 1951 to 1971 period.

Student enrollment increased from 5,000 students in 1951 to 25,000 in 1971. A commensurate increase in the faculty also occurred. The Wilkinson period continued the recruitment of strong faculty with graduate degrees from major American universities. Student services expanded, student housing mushroomed, and a city was built on Temple Hill. Perhaps the most important event during the Wilkinson administration was the creation of student wards and stakes. This one spark of inspiration has had enormous impact on the entire campus community.

Elder Neal A. Maxwell, speaking as Church commissioner of education at the time of President Wilkinson's resignation, said of him: "This is the man who too often is remembered for the brick-and-mortar growth of this institution when in fact its major thrust has been in the direction of quality and excellence. For this he deserves, I think, much of the credit for what has happened here in the making of a university."[16]

Speaking of the Wilkinson years after becoming president of the university himself, Elder Dallin H. Oaks stated that BYU "would probably still be struggling around the fringes of community college status had it not been for the remarkable and relentless leadership of the Wilkinson Era."[17]

1971–1999: A Time of Excellence

Student enrollment caps came into existence in the mid-1970s. Consequently, physical growth has not been a major factor in university life during the last twenty-five years. It has allowed the faculty, staff, and administrations to focus on the quality of the offerings as well as the quality of the facilities. Early in his administration, President Dallin H. Oaks indicated that he had two objectives. The first was to "reinforce the University's drive for excellence as an academic institution" and the second was to "preserve the distinctive spiritual character and standards of the University.[18]

University presidents since 1971 have been charged with the dual responsibility of improving learning in both sacred and secular realms. The expectation is that the university will excel in both. Building testimonies is as much a part of this university as teaching chemistry. Brigham Young University is an integral part of the Church and is expected to play a role in building the kingdom. President Harold B. Lee, in his charge to President Oaks in 1971, stated: "Brigham Young University, led by its President, must never forget its role in bringing to reality the ancient prophecy—to build the mountain of the Lord's house in the tops of the mountains, so great and so glorious that all nations may come to this place and be constrained to say 'show us your way that we may walk therein.' (See Isaiah 2:3.)"[19]

The Present

Given the incredible history of this institution, where do we stand today? The data indicate that improvement across campus is continuing, and the university, like a flower, is through the budding stage and has begun to show its beauty. The quality and beauty of our programs are capturing attention, and our creative works, as well as our graduates, are making a difference in the world. During the past year a set of institutional objectives were proposed that I would like to share with you. I will use the objectives to illustrate the status of the university. The objectives are not new, as noted earlier. They are implied by BYU's Mission Statement written in the 1980s and the aims formulated in this decade [the 1990s]. In a succinct manner they outline the standards and aspirations set for the university by the board of trustees.

First Institutional Objective

The first objective is concerned with the quality of teaching at Brigham Young University. The objective relates to the four aims and reads as follows:

Educate the minds and spirits of students within a learning environment that

- increases faith in God and the restored gospel,
- is intellectually enlarging,
- is character building,
- and leads to a life of learning and service.

Evidence regarding the quality of teaching at BYU comes in many forms. Two recent surveys are informative with respect to the spiritual, intellectual, and character offerings of the faculty and staff and their impact on students. The first relates to the spiritual offering and was administered at Brigham Young University this past year by Keith Wilson of Religious Education in tandem with two professors from Baylor University. This survey of BYU faculty compared results from similar church-related institutions such as

Baylor, Notre Dame, and Boston College. The researchers sought to analyze the influence of religion in an academic setting. One part of the survey assessed the willingness of faculty to share their beliefs in the classroom. One of the questions asked faculty how they felt about expressing certain Christian behaviors on campus.

The behaviors included a willingness to discuss gospel-related questions when those questions are raised by class materials; a willingness to share religious experiences in class; a willingness to lead a class in prayer; and a willingness to bear testimony. The faculty surveyed were asked to respond to each category.

My purpose in using the data is not to compare the BYU faculty responses with those from other campuses but to look at the extraordinarily high percentage of "yes" answers received. Ninety-nine percent of the BYU faculty surveyed indicated a willingness to answer gospel-related questions raised by class materials. Ninety-two percent of the faculty currently do share or are willing to share personal experiences that have a faith component. More than four out of five are willing to lead the class in prayer. Finally, nine out of ten faculty members are willing to bear witness of their personal testimony of the restored gospel. The last question was not asked of faculty at the other universities.

I believe these extraordinary responses reflect the faithfulness of the faculty and their commitment to the mission of Brigham Young University. I also believe that the faithfulness of the faculty and staff are reflected in the answers received in a recent survey of our graduates of three years ago.

• I had a science teacher who told us that our purpose at BYU is to figure out our relationship with God. You know, that was his encouragement. And he spent like a whole hour one day talking on it. And as far as even my beliefs as being LDS, I think he was

right. The whole BYU experience is there for young people to figure out who they are in relationship with their God. And I think
between the wards and between intellectual and social development, I think it can do that if you apply the system right.

• I came from a small town where there were only a few members. I'd never been around so many Church members in all my
life, and I started to understand the Church in a different way. It's
kind of like having a picture of the Church in my head to take
away with me, irrespective of where I go.

• My wife and I had our first daughter at BYU, and we
decided that we would both continue to go to school. . . . And I
don't know if we could have done that at many other schools, but
I remember a couple of examples of how BYU helped us. I guess it
positively contributed to our family. We had tried to work out
schedules so . . . one of us would watch our daughter while the
other one was in class. There were a couple of times when that
didn't work out. One time my wife had to take a quiz, but she had
to have our daughter with her. And our daughter was one month
old. Our baby started crying during the middle of that Russian
quiz. The teacher went over, picked our daughter up, took her
outside, and rocked her to sleep. Anyway, this teacher is one of the
most world-renowned guys as far as Russian studies go . . . , and I
cannot get that out of my mind, thinking that he was taking care
of my daughter so my wife could learn. I think he really had the
good picture, realizing that family and education don't have to
conflict with each other—they can help each other.

The academic quality of BYU is becoming known outside
Provo. Most have seen the issue of the *U.S. News and World
Report* that gave the magazine's annual assessment of the various
institutions that make up higher education.[20]

We are pleased with the rankings that had both the J. Reuben

Clark Law School and the Marriott School of Management among the top fifty in the United States. The more recent rankings place the business school and the College of Engineering among the nation's best, with the university at large ranking in the second tier. Due to marginal improvements in a number of categories, the overall ranking for BYU among 1,400 institutions of higher education and 228 major research universities jumped significantly from 109th last year to 80th this year. Improvement occurred in the freshman retention rate, the graduation rate, faculty resources, student selectivity, financial resources, and the alumni giving rate.

I first came to the university thirty-two years ago. At the time there were pockets of excellence on campus. I left BYU in the early 1970s and returned in the late seventies. I noticed a significant improvement as program strength was more widespread. Today every program is one of quality with a strong and productive faculty. Staff quality has improved as additional resources have been made available by the board of trustees. Please do not misinterpret my statements. We have not arrived! There is more to do! But we have vision, commitment, and additional resources—these are the ingredients that will move us forward.

Second Institutional Objective

The second institutional objective concerns the quality of research performed at BYU. It is my firm opinion that a major university must contribute to the world's storehouse of knowledge. Also, we believe that the research and creative efforts should be consequential; that is, they should make a difference. With this in mind, the second objective reads as follows:

Advance truth and knowledge to
• enhance the education of students
• enrich the quality of life
• and contribute to a resolution of world problems.

The second objective will be fulfilled if our research involves students and improves their education directly or indirectly; if the creative works in the fine arts and humanities capture or add beauty to this world; if the theoretical research performed in the laboratory provides a clearer understanding of how things work; if the research and creative efforts in the biological, social, health, physical, and engineering sciences and in law and business improve the world in some way.

The deans have supplied me with many examples of consequential scholarship by a number of scholars in almost every department. I have selected three. The danger is that my selection will stereotype what is meant by important research. Please recognize that my selection is limited.

The first is a study of families with children with disabilities. An interdisciplinary team of BYU faculty from nursing, family sciences, and education have followed a group of families with children with disabilities for the past five years. Their work has been nationally and internationally recognized as an important effort to understand the role of all family members in the significant experience of raising a child with a disability. Data include important insights related to areas of stress as well as areas of family growth, including the power of religious faith.

The second example comes from the clinical psychology faculty, where three professors through a long-term project have produced a reliable and inexpensive test to measure the level of depression in human beings. The questionnaire is currently used by HMOs, government agencies, and state hospital systems covering millions of individuals. The advantages of the instrument, which has been exhaustively tested, include quicker detection—reducing the costs of treatment—and its unique ability to measure the effect of ongoing therapy or medication on the level of illness.

The third example comes from the College of Engineering, where a number of faculty are engaged in pioneering research into configurable computing. One article in *Scientific American* indicated that the work at BYU places the university among the top five in the world with respect to this type of research.[21]

Third Institutional Objective

The third institutional objective is concerned with the influence that BYU may have in blessing LDS members around the world. The objective reads:

Extend the blessings of learning to members of the Church in all parts of the world.

With 1.5 million 18- to 25-year-olds in the Church and a significant portion who would like to attend BYU, it is obvious that only a tiny fraction can be served on campus. Moreover, the proportion served will decline over time. Some will attend other universities where they can take institute classes. Others will not have the opportunity to study. What are the ways in which this university can reach out and bless them?

First, two steps already have been taken on campus to accommodate more students. The first is the 2,000 FTE student increase in the enrollment cap. Obviously, this is a small step. The second is the visiting student or open enrollment program for the spring and summer semesters. This will allow a few thousand more students to come.

Other steps taken include the development of an Internet curriculum to complement and eventually replace the pencil and paper courses of Independent Study. A year ago BYU had 20 courses on-line. The number today is 117. Of this number, approximately 20 are high school courses. For some countries the high school courses are more critical than the college materials. During the next three or four years another 200 or more courses will be added. The best part of the Internet course development is that teams of faculty from various departments are working on the large general education courses. The first priority is to develop high-quality course materials for on-campus students. A family history course produced by Susan Easton Black recently received the national UCEA award (University Continuing Education Association) for one of the best courses designed in 1999. A panel of judges carefully reviewed a large number of courses before giving the award.

A new bachelor of general studies has been approved by the appropriate faculty committees. This degree replaces the bachelor of independent study program. With the appropriate number of residence hours, students who leave the university without graduating can complete a degree over the Internet. Of the 300,000 alumni, approximately 150,000 did not graduate. Continuing Education personnel recently stratified the nongraduates by the number of hours completed on campus. There were more than 600 former students with more than 140 hours of credit but no degree. The first set of letters inviting alumni to finish were sent to them. The second letter of invitation will go to those with 120 hours or more, and so on. The program was announced a few months ago, and there are now 713 active registrants in the new BGS program and 1,000 who have applied.

The usual scenario one thinks of when considering instruction over the Internet is a student at home taking a course. A more important option in distant places is for a group of students taking courses together under the direction of a mentor. Currently the Church Educational System is conducting experiments with pilot programs in Brazil and Mexico. One can think of circumstances where BYU students could assist through a service/learning internship. This was tried in Brazil and Mexico during the summer with approximately four students in each country. We are evaluating their experience presently.

The foreign groups may take courses not to complete a degree but to obtain a set of skills that will enable them to improve their employability. Or using the courseware may open the door for entrance to a university in their country. Recently I met with the senior executives of one of the largest multinational corporations in the world. They are in the midst of major expansion plans in Central and South America. I asked the executives if they would be interested in hiring natives in those countries who had spent the last two years in a highly disciplined program where they arose every morning at 6:30, studied written materials for two hours, spent 10 to 12 hours per day meeting people and trying to explain their beliefs, learned to handle rejection, had developed strong oral communication skills, and were totally honest in their dealings. Moreover, they were now in a program learning English as a second language and becoming proficient in the use of the computer. The first response was one of disbelief. The second was a commitment to work with Church employment people in those countries to hire returned missionaries.

There are many ways in which Brigham Young University can extend the blessings of learning across the world. Technology is opening the door for high-quality instruction and interaction that will cut across geographical boundaries and cultures.

Fourth Institutional Objective

The final objective relates to nonmembers. The objective is: **Develop friends** for the university and the Church.

Friends of the faculty and staff quickly learn about the quality of the university. Research ties between BYU faculty and faculty of other institutions are important in the development of friends in the academic community. Collaboration on research and conferences is much easier today because of improvements in communications. National and international conferences also allow the staff to present papers on their work at BYU. Again, their counterparts learn about innovations at BYU. A number of BYU administrative staff are considered leaders in their areas.

For many years BYU's performing groups have been ambassadors for the Church and the university. So far, in 1999, 644 BYU students have presented 336 concerts in 160 cities in 13 countries. Approximately 330,000 people watched the live performances, and another 35.5 million saw them on television.[22]

BYU's ambassadorial program brings foreign ambassadors to campus at a rate of two or three per semester. They speak to an assemblage in the Kennedy Center and meet students from their country as well as returned missionaries who served there. They meet with members of the First Presidency and Quorum of the Twelve. They see this magnificent campus and learn about us as a people.

These are the four objectives. May I suggest a word of caution. The key focus must be the *quality* of on-campus education. If our attention is diverted away from the first and second objectives to the third and fourth, the foundation of excellence will be eroded and the university will fail to reach its potential. It is important to understand that the third and fourth objectives will be realized if we are successful in achieving the first two. If the light on campus becomes a "standard for the nations," then the outside world will be attracted to us. The first two objectives involve everyone in one way or another and should occupy a very large fraction of our time. In contrast, the third and fourth objectives are derivatives, and only a few people will be directly involved.

The Future: World-Class, Worldwide

With an extraordinary faculty, highly qualified students, resources from the board, and support from private donations to help us improve, the small seed planted in 1875 is maturing into a beautiful, white tree—one whose fruit is delicious to the taste, one that will shine as a standard for the nations because of its dual nature. For the first time I see a world-class, worldwide university as a reality. We have not arrived! In this lifetime we will never be fully satisfied. There is still much work to be done! But the quality is coming and the influence is spreading.

In closing, may I share a recent experience. A short time ago I got a call from Elder Jeffrey R. Holland indicating that he had just received an assignment to accompany a friend of the First Presidency on a visit to BYU. The individual in question is a well-known leader in Asia and heads one of the largest Muslim groups in the world—a group totaling 40 million members. The leader had learned about BYU's first translation of an Islamic work: *The Incoherence of the Philosophers by Al-Ghazali.*[23]

Accompanying the leader was a visiting professor at Harvard and a prominent Asian businessman. Following a luncheon and a campus tour, both expressed surprise at the beauty, size, and cleanliness of the campus. They were not aware that BYU is the largest private university in the United States, that students come from each state in the Union and from more than 100 foreign countries. They were amazed to learn that more than 60 languages are taught on campus and more than 80 are spoken. Discussions were held regarding the possibility of further visits, student exchanges, and the recruiting of BYU students for employment.

As the visitors left, I thought how important BYU is as a window on the Church. The glass is not dark but clear and allows viewers to see the values and truths of the restored gospel. Through this window nonmembers feel the importance of education to Church members. They see the youth of the Church, note their strength, and observe the peace within them. The veil that separates is thin when they meet with faculty, discern their cultural sensitivities, and sense the quality of their work and thought.

How grateful I am for Brigham Young University, for the assemblage of faculty, staff, and students gathered here. I appreciate even more deeply the special role played by BYU in addition to its fundamental purpose of educating young people. It is an integral part of the kingdom of God on earth. It is an important arm of the Church in helping the world come to an understanding of who the LDS people are and of the values and light that we treasure.

NOTES

1. In Alma P. Burton, *Karl G. Maeser: Mormon Educator* (Salt Lake City: Deseret Book Company, 1953), 26.

2. Ernest L. Wilkinson and W. Cleon Skousen, *Brigham Young University: A School of Destiny* (Provo, Utah: Brigham Young University Press, 1976), 46–47.

3. Wilkinson and Skousen, *Brigham Young University,* 46.

4. Wilkinson and Skousen, *Brigham Young University,* 47; text modernized.

5. Wilkinson and Skousen, *Brigham Young University,* 48.

6. Wilkinson and Skousen, *Brigham Young University,* 118–19.

7. Wilkinson and Skousen, *Brigham Young University*, 83.

8. Wilkinson and Skousen, *Brigham Young University*, 164–65.

9. Wilkinson and Skousen, *Brigham Young University*, 135; see also 755.

10. Wilkinson and Skousen, *Brigham Young University*, 130.

11. Wilkinson and Skousen, *Brigham Young University*, 190–91.

12. Wilkinson and Skousen, *Brigham Young University*, 193.

13. Wilkinson and Skousen, *Brigham Young University*, 254.

14. "Vision of Dr. Sidney B. Sperry," A Memorandum by W. Cleon Skousen, September 24, 1975, Brigham Young University Archives, 1.

15. "Vision of Dr. Sidney B. Sperry," 2.

16. Wilkinson and Skousen, *Brigham Young University*, 759.

17. Wilkinson and Skousen, *Brigham Young University*, 759.

18. Wilkinson and Skousen, *Brigham Young University*, 779.

19. Harold B. Lee, "Installation of and Charge to the President," in *Educating Zion,* eds. John W. Welch and Don E. Norton (Provo, Utah: BYU Studies, 1996), 93.

20. See "Best Colleges 2000," *U.S. News and World Report* 127, no. 8 (30 August 1999): 84–105.

21. See John Villasenor and William H. Mangione-Smith, "Configurable Computing," *Scientific American* (June 1997): 66–71.

22. See "Goodwil Ambassadors," *Church News,* 21 August 1999, 8–10.

23. Al-Ghazali, *The Incoherence of the Philosophers.* Translated, introduced, and annotated by Michael E. Marmura (Provo, Utah: Brigham Young University Press, 1997).

CHAPTER 5

A Peculiar Treasure

(3 SEPTEMBER 1996)

IT IS WONDERFUL to contemplate the bright countenances and gospel light that enervates the souls of the students at Brigham Young University. Seeing them reminds me of the Israelites' experience when Moses returned from Mount Sinai after spending forty days and nights with the Lord. During his time on the mount, Moses fasted, neither eating bread nor drinking water as he recorded the Lord's instructions on the tables of stone (see Exodus 34:28). As he descended the mountain and approached the camp, the scriptures record that "the skin of his face shone" and "Aaron and all the children of Israel . . . were afraid to come nigh him" (Exodus 34:29–30).

The light emanating from these students is reminiscent of the experiences Sister Bateman and I had in Japan and Korea during 1993–94. Shortly after our arrival in Japan, we attended a district conference in northern Honshu. Arrangements were made before the trip for a member of the district presidency, a brother whom we did not know, to meet us at the train station. As the bullet train sped from Tokyo to Morioka, I wondered how we would recognize the Japanese brother. The train station would be a beehive of activity. It would be easier for him to recognize us than the reverse, but there would be hundreds of people exiting the train. Stepping from the train car onto the platform, I looked into a sea of Japanese faces, wondering which one was there to greet us. As we gazed along the platform, I could see an individual at the far end whose countenance radiated the light of the gospel. He was checking each car as he passed along the platform. As we moved toward him, he recognized us, and a peaceful feeling entered our souls. That experience was repeated almost weekly as we met unknown Japanese and Korean brothers and sisters in busy airport terminals and train stations from Sapporo to Fukuoka, from Seoul to Pusan. The warmth of the gospel light radiating from these brothers and sisters was the identifying characteristic that brought us together.

You are part of an elect family—the Lord's covenant people. When Abraham was ninety-nine years old, the Lord appeared to him and said: "I am the Almighty God; walk before me. . . . And I will establish my covenant between me and thee and thy seed after thee . . . for an everlasting covenant, to be a God unto thee, and to thy seed after thee" (Genesis 17:1, 7).

In exchange for Abraham's righteousness, the Lord promised him the blessings of the gospel, a land, and a large posterity (see Genesis 12–13; Abraham 1:16–19). In order to fulfill the covenant, the Lord gave Abraham a son through Sarah and a righteous posterity through Isaac's lineage. Abraham received the fullness of the gospel and was told that gospel covenants and blessings would be offered to his children and his children's children (see D&C 132:29–50; Abraham 2:6–11).

I am impressed with the power of knowing and having faith

in one's relationship to Abraham and Sarah, to Isaac and Jacob, to Joseph and his brothers. We are Israel! We are inheritors of the Lord's promises to our ancient forefathers. One of the most powerful and distinguishing doctrines of the restored gospel is the notion that the Bible is about us, that we are part of the biblical narrative. Although the rest of Christianity applies Bible teachings to their lives, it is our belief that the Bible was written by our ancestors, who saw our day and left messages for us. Isaiah, Jeremiah, Ezekiel, and other prophets saw in vision the restoration of the gospel in the last days, the gathering of Israel, the stretching of the Lord's tent across the earth, the building of latter-day Zion and its temples, and stakes being established and strengthened as a refuge from the storm (see Isaiah 2:2–3; 29; 54:2–4; Jeremiah 29:14; 31; 32:37–40; Ezekiel 37:15–23).

During the course of history there have been a number of occasions when righteous Abrahamic descendants have enjoyed living under the gospel covenant. Whenever the Lord has had a covenant people on earth, a special term has been applied to them. They are called "a peculiar treasure" (Exodus 19:5; see also 1 Peter 2:9). In what ways are righteous people peculiar? There are at least three differentiating characteristics.

First, they believe in and have a greater knowledge of God and His Son. They not only believe in a supreme being but come to know and trust Him.

Second, the trust in Deity helps them live differently from others as they abide gospel principles. Obedience to God's ways produces a clean, happy people. This in turn leads to a special bonding among them. Students on this campus come from more than 100 nations. As you meet, we believe that shared gospel beliefs will be stronger than cultural differences that may divide.

Third, a covenant people not only believe in God but are

sensitive to spiritual things through the power of the Holy Ghost. I sensed this peculiarity once when 5,000 freshmen gathered in this hall. One moment they were singing loudly "Rise and Shout" with the Pep Band. The next moment they were listening quietly and intently, feeling the power of the Spirit as Professor Paul Cox explained "The Aims of a BYU Education." One could feel the spiritual depth and commitment of the entering class.

As covenant children of the Lord and as His peculiar treasure, we must strengthen continually our faith in Him and in His atonement. Alma's discourse on faith clearly teaches that it is not enough to turn the seed into a small seedling. That is the first step, but one must continue the nurturing process until the word has become the tree of life within one's soul (see Alma 32:27–43). Also, if covenant children are to take advantage of the educational opportunities provided by this university, they must follow the Lord's counsel to Joseph Smith regarding the learning process. May I discuss these two topics in reverse order—the learning process first, followed by a witness of the Savior's atonement.

Diligence and Obedience

The students at this university have broader objectives than most students elsewhere. Many are seeking sacred as well as secular truth. You have chosen Brigham Young University knowing the dual nature of the institution. A few months ago I received a letter from a young woman who expressed her feelings in this regard. She said:

> I especially am grateful for the emphasis . . . placed on BYU being a religious institution. I'm from central California and was the valedictorian of my high school

class. I felt a lot of pressure from teachers and peers to attend an Ivy League school, Stanford, or one of the more prestigious University of California schools. They could not understand why I would even consider BYU—let alone choose it above the others! But in my mind, I knew the importance of educating my spirit as well as my brain. I wanted a religious education as well as a secular one. I knew that BYU was a place that could provide this type of experience. Since entering here [last] fall, this hope has been confirmed, and I have grown in so many ways that would never have been possible at another university.[1]

Whether sacred or secular, the process of acquiring truth follows the same basic pattern. The Lord said, "All things unto me are spiritual, and not at any time have I given unto you a law [truth] which was temporal" (D&C 29:34). Whether one attempts to learn by faith or by study, the learning process is similar in at least two respects. First, learning is based on diligence—the energetic application of one's mental powers. Second, the acquisition of knowledge and intelligence is based on one's obedience to basic truths. The scriptures state: "Whatever principle of intelligence we attain unto in this life, it will rise with us in the resurrection. And if a person gains more knowledge and intelligence in this life through his diligence and obedience than another, he will have so much the advantage in the world to come" (D&C 130:18–19).

Oliver Cowdery learned this lesson when he was given the opportunity to assist Joseph in translating the plates. He was unable to do so, and the Lord explained why:

"Behold, you have not understood; you have supposed that I

would give it unto you, when you took no thought save it was to ask me.

"But, behold, I say unto you, that you must study it out in your mind; then you must ask me if it be right, and if it is right I will cause that your bosom shall burn within you; therefore, you shall feel that it is right" (D&C 9:7–8).

Whether it is called diligence, hard work, or effort, consistent application of one's energy is required to learn. As an undergraduate student, good grades came easily for me. My diligence was generally confined to class time plus the night before the exam. There were only a few classes that caused me to stretch. Looking back, I now realize how I squandered a major opportunity.

In contrast, graduate school was a different experience. When I arrived at the Massachusetts Institute of Technology, I realized that I was not prepared and had shortchanged myself as an undergraduate. I was three years behind in mathematics and not well prepared in my major. It took eighteen hours a day, six days a week, of study and class time to compete with the better students. While taking courses in my chosen field, I also studied calculus and difference and differential equations, plus linear algebra—tools required to pass the major exams. During the first year in graduate school I came to understand the meaning of the word *diligence*. I vowed then to apply my energies in whatever pursuit I was engaged and not waste opportunities.

Just as the secular learning process requires diligence, so does the search for sacred truths. The Prophet Joseph Smith stated: "When a man works by faith he works by mental exertion instead of physical force."[2] In other words, sacred knowledge or a witness of the Spirit comes only after the expenditure of significant mental energy.

A few years ago, a returned missionary who served in one of

the Mexican missions shared with me a classic experience that illustrates the "diligence" principle in the acquisition of faith and sacred knowledge. I had conducted the stake president's interview before his mission and sent his papers to Church headquarters. I remember that interview with him. He was 6 foot 5 inches tall and 255 pounds. He was one of the first two young men recruited from my children's high school to play football at Brigham Young University. He was a fine young man, clean-cut and worthy in every way. I remember being impressed with his potential. I could tell from the answers he gave to the questions I asked that he was honest, but there was one crack in his armor. I knew that his testimony was based on the faith of others rather than on his own witness. In contrast, he related the following story to me during his release interview at the end of his mission.

As his mission began, Elder Stone worked energetically with his companion. Frequently he was called upon to give the first lesson. In the lesson it was necessary for him to tell the investigators about the appearance of the Father and the Son to the boy Joseph in the Sacred Grove and then bear witness of its truthfulness. After bearing testimony a number of times, his conscience began to bother him. Although he *believed* the story, he did not *know* that it actually happened. He had not been there, nor had he received a witness that it had occurred. How could he tell others that the First Vision really happened? As doubts began to multiply and replace his belief and as the pains of conscience increased, he told his companion that he could no longer be a missionary. He was going home. He could not serve as a witness to something he did not know. His companion responded, "Elder Stone, why don't you follow the counsel given the investigators? You need to study and pray more diligently. Put Moroni's promise to the test.

Exercise your faith, and you will receive an answer. Stay with me for a few more weeks."

Elder Stone agreed to stay and put Moroni's promise to the test. A few weeks passed, the missionary worked harder, prayed more often, was more attentive in his reading, but no witness came. Finally, during an interview with the mission president, Elder Stone expressed his frustrations and indicated his desire to return home. He could not continue. A wise mission president counseled, "Elder, do not give up! You have a desire to believe. If you continue faithful in your calling for a few more weeks, the Lord will answer your prayers. I promise you!"

Elder Stone agreed to return to his proselyting area for a few more weeks. Again, days and then weeks passed with no change in his feelings. It was difficult. One morning as they were knocking on doors, a woman answered and invited them to return when her husband and children would be home. As they left the small house, Elder Stone said to his companion, "I'm not giving the lesson!"

His companion responded, "Elder, I'll give the first portion of the discussion, but I want you to tell the Joseph Smith story."

Finally Elder Stone agreed, even though that was the part that bothered him. From the time they left the woman's house until they returned a day or two later, the missionary used every spare minute to read and pray. He wanted a witness before entering the home. But when the appointed hour came, he still had not received a witness. He had read diligently, he had prayed almost continuously, but there were no special feelings. How could he bear witness when he did not know?

The father answered the door and ushered the missionaries inside. There on a dirt floor sat nine children, and the father and mother took their places behind them. Elder Stone reported that the size of the home was not much larger than his bedroom in Utah. The humble circumstances only added to his discomfort. The senior companion began the lesson, telling the family that there is a God, that we are His children, and that He loves us. He then explained the mission of the Savior, how God sent His Son to earth to atone for our sins and to make possible our return to our heavenly home. He explained the role of prophets and bore witness that God works through prophets today. He then turned the lesson over to Elder Stone.

My missionary friend began the story of the fourteen-year-old Joseph. He told the family about the religious confusion that existed in Palmyra in the 1820s, how Joseph listened to the various ministers proclaiming different versions of Christianity. He told them about Joseph's experience in reading James 1:5, where James states unequivocally: "If any of you lack wisdom, let him ask of God, that giveth to all men liberally, and upbraideth not; and it shall be given him" (James 1:5).

The missionary related the impact that the passage had on Joseph—that it struck him with more power than had any other scripture, and that this caused him to reflect on it again and again. Finally, Joseph decided to put James to the test. He selected a grove of trees near his father's farm and went there on a beautiful spring day to pray. Being alone, he knelt down and offered up the feelings of his heart. The elder told the family how a dark power came over Joseph, almost choking the life out of the young boy. Exerting all of his powers, Joseph continued to pray, and then, suddenly, a pillar of light descended out of the heavens directly above him. The darkness was dispelled, and in the midst of the light were two personages. One called Joseph by name and, pointing to the other, said: "This is My Beloved Son. Hear Him!" (See Joseph Smith–History 1:1–17.)

At this point in the story, Elder Stone said that a warm feeling began to stir his soul—one he had never felt before. The warmth was deep inside and soon enveloped him. Tears welled up in his eyes. His throat became full, and he could hardly speak. He was embarrassed and ducked his head until he could regain his composure. When he looked up, he noticed tears in the eyes of the parents and the children. They were experiencing the same feelings and warmth of Spirit that he was feeling. He finished the lesson with a conviction born of a spiritual witness that Joseph Smith saw the Father and the Son. Elder Stone's testimony had shifted from one of belief to a knowledge of the First Vision. As Elder Stone finished sharing his experience with me, he said: "President, I know that Joseph saw the Father and the Son. I did not have a problem in the mission field after that experience. I have my own witness."

As I listened to the story's conclusion, I thought how efficient God is: he got twelve birds with one Stone! The parents, the nine children, and a missionary were all touched by the Holy Ghost, and a desire to believe was transformed into knowledge. More than that, God is efficient in another way. If a person has a witness of the Father and Son's visit to young Joseph, he or she has a foundation for believing and accepting other gospel principles. The Word of Wisdom, tithing, the law of chastity, and all other principles revealed through the Prophet Joseph Smith are true. Once one feels the good seed growing and swelling inside, one has a small amount of knowledge that forms the basis for further growth. In the words of Alma:

"And now, behold, is your knowledge perfect? Yea, your knowledge is perfect in that thing, and your faith is dormant; and this because you know, for ye know that the word hath swelled your souls, and ye also know that it hath sprouted up, that your understanding doth begin to be enlightened, and your mind doth begin to expand" (Alma 32:34).

The important aspect of the story for us is the diligence required of Elder Stone. The answer did not come the first time he prayed or the second or the third. Weeks went by as his faith and desires were tested. As Moroni states: "Faith is things which are hoped for and not seen; wherefore, dispute not because ye see not, for ye receive no witness until after the trial of your faith" (Ether 12:6).

A Witness of Christ

May I share with you my witness of the divinity of the Lord Jesus Christ. His atonement in the meridian of time is the most important event in human history. I know that in a garden Adam and Eve fell that you and I might experience mortality. I also know that in another garden and on the cross, the Lord and Creator of this earth suffered our sins so that we can return home if we will exercise faith in Him and repent. There are many scriptures that have helped me understand the personal nature of the Atonement. Two are exceptional. The first is from Alma 7:11–12:

"And he shall go forth, suffering pains and afflictions and temptations of every kind; and this that the word might be fulfilled which saith he will take upon him the pains and the sicknesses of his people.

"And he will take upon him death, that he may loose the bands of death which bind his people; and he will take upon him their infirmities, that his bowels may be filled with mercy, according to the flesh, that he may know according to the flesh how to succor his people according to their infirmities."

Alma reveals to us the process by which the Master learned

perfect empathy in the flesh. He experienced not only our sins but also our pains, sufferings, temptations of every kind, sicknesses, infirmities, and weaknesses. He also experienced death in order to loose the bands of death for His people. Consequently, if one of us has a special problem, it is not possible for him or her to say, "No one knows what I am experiencing. No one understands my pain or suffering." The Lord knows! He not only knows the depth of your experience, He knows how to succor you because of His suffering.

The second passage comes from Mosiah, where the prophet Abinadi quotes chapter 53 of Isaiah to the wicked priests of King Noah:

"And now I say unto you, who shall declare his generation? Behold, I say unto you, that when his soul has been made an offering for sin he shall see his seed. And now what say ye? And who shall be his seed?

"Behold I say unto you, that whosoever has heard the words of the prophets [and has] hearkened unto their words, and believed that the Lord would redeem his people . . . are his seed" (Mosiah 15:10–11).

For many years I envisioned the Garden of Gethsemane and the cross as places where an infinite mass of sin and pain were heaped upon the Savior. Thanks to Alma and Abinadi, it is no longer an infinite mass but an infinite stream of people with whom the Savior became intimately acquainted as He suffered our sins, pains, and afflictions. I testify that He knows each of us, is concerned about our progress, and has the infinite capacity not only to heal our wounds but also to lift us up to the Father as sanctified sons and daughters.

NOTES

1. Personal correspondence, February 1996.
2. N. B. Lundwall, comp., *Lectures on Faith* (Salt Lake City: Bookcraft, n.d.), 61 [7:3].

FAITH, HOPE, AND CHARITY

CHAPTER 6

A Faith That Preserves and Strengthens

(7 JANUARY 1997)

THE FIRST PRINCIPLE of the gospel is faith in the Lord Jesus Christ. This principle is fundamental to the way we think and act. It defines the set of beliefs and motivations not only for members of the Church but for us as a university community. It explains why most of us have chosen to be here. It is the basis for the university code by which we try to live. Our faith pushes us to do our best not only for ourselves but to make this institution better. It provides the cohesiveness that makes the whole greater than the sum of the parts.

Faith is both a principle and a process. It defines the path by which we build a relationship of trust with the Savior. In order for faith to develop, we must begin with a humble heart and contrite spirit, have a strong desire to know the Lord, and then be obedient to gospel principles. In return, the Savior rewards the obedient with spiritual confirmations of their actions (see Alma 32:16, 27–32). As faith grows, our vision of eternity expands, which increases our capacity to meet life's challenges. As we become more familiar with the Lord's plan of happiness, we understand that trials and adversity occur for many reasons and are a part of the testing and growth process.

Both ancient and modern-day prophets have taught that mortality is a probationary state—a time of testing—and that the Lord gives us experiences to enable us to grow (see Abraham 3:25–26; Proverbs 3:11–12; Alma 42:4). Some of life's events cause heartache and pain. If our faith in the Lord is weak, the probability is high that we will not learn the lessons intended. Elder Richard G. Scott spoke about the relationship between faith and adversity in the October 1995 general conference.[1] He suggested that when adversity strikes, there is a natural tendency to feel sorry for ourselves and to waste energy wondering why such adversity has come upon us. In contrast, if our faith in the Lord and His plan is strong, we will accept the adversity and try to learn from it. This opens the door for the Holy Spirit to work within us, increasing our faith and bestowing upon us divine gifts. Elder Scott further stated: "This life is an experience in profound trust—trust in Jesus Christ, trust in His teachings, trust in our capacity as led by the Holy Spirit to obey those teachings. . . . To produce fruit, your trust in the Lord must be more powerful and enduring than your confidence in your own personal feelings and experience."[2]

As our faith in the Lord grows, we can put aside our own desires and feelings and submit to the Lord's will. There are many accounts of faithful souls who have faced adversity and through faith in Christ have met the challenges and emerged victors. Let us explore the meaning of the term *faith* as defined by the Apostle Paul and the Prophet Joseph Smith and then illustrate the preserving and strengthening power of faith with three examples—the first two from the life of an ancient patriarch and the third from a modern-day story of a young girl and her family.

Paul's Definition of Faith

Chapter 11 of Paul's epistle to the Hebrews is devoted to the principle of faith. After defining the term as "the substance of things hoped for, the evidence of things not seen" (v. 1), the apostle cites a number of events from the Old Testament that exemplify faith. In particular, Paul uses these stories to teach the Jewish members of the Church about faith and how the faith of the ancient prophets was centered in Jesus Christ.

Although I used this scripture as a missionary to explain to investigators the concept of faith, I did not grasp fully the meaning of Paul's succinct statement, and I suspect that many of my investigators wondered as well. Further, I did not sufficiently appreciate the lessons of faith taught by the illustrations that followed his definition.

A few years ago I discovered that Joseph Smith made a simple change in Paul's statement when the Prophet translated the Bible. In the Joseph Smith Translation, the Prophet changed the word *substance* to *assurance*. Thus the JST definition reads: "Now faith is the *assurance* of things hoped for, the evidence of things not seen" (JST, Hebrews 11:1; emphasis added). The word *assurance* provides insight as to the foundation upon which faith is built. It suggests that the underpinning of our faith or belief is an internal, spiritual witness. The word *substance* suggests something tangible. The word *assurance* indicates a spiritual affirmation of the "things hoped for." As Moroni promised, belief and works will be followed by a witness of the Spirit (see Moroni 10:3–5).

In my early years I was confused by the fact that some

individuals read the Book of Mormon, prayed about it, and received the witness promised, but others seemed to follow the same course but never received the witness. I have since learned that it is not God who is random but we mortals. Some individuals don't believe they will receive a spiritual prompting even though they may pray. Others are not diligent in applying the truths they have been taught. An important lesson of life is to learn that the Father and the Son deliver on Their promises, but we must do our part.

We should remember, however, that the Holy Ghost's witness comes after the trial of faith and not necessarily on our time schedule (see Galatians 3:14; 2 Corinthians 1:22; 5:5; Ephesians 1:13–14; Ether 12:6). In Alma's explanation of the process, the experiment of faith begins with a humble heart combined with a desire to believe. This is followed by the planting and nurturing of the seed, and then come the "swelling motions" and enlightened understanding (see Alma 32:27–32). Alma does not specify how long the planting and nurturing process takes. For some the season may be short. For others more time may be required for the lessons to be learned. Because of the internal nature of the witness, the evidence is not seen or seeable by others except when they follow the same process.

When a witness is received, is that the end? No! There are still many lessons to be learned and fruits of the Spirit to be received. An investigator who has felt the initial promptings of the Holy Ghost does not know all there is to know about the gospel. But a foundation has been laid for his or her spiritual growth. Spiritual confirmation becomes an integral part of a person's faith; it becomes an anchor for a more sure hope (see Ether 12:4) and leads men and women to higher and deeper levels of faith as they continue to "nourish the word . . . with great diligence" (Alma

32:41). When we understand that faith matures over time through belief, obedience, and witness, Joseph's substitution of *assurance* for *substance* is meaningful.

Paul's Examples of Faith

In Hebrews 11, Paul cites many examples of faith from the lives of ancient prophets and patriarchs. The events taken from the lives of these great leaders illustrate the preserving and strengthening power of faith. Paul begins with Abel's sacrifice, followed by other examples from the lives of Enoch, Noah, Abraham, and others. Paul shows how each prophet's faith is rooted in Christ. In order to understand the centrality of Christ and the Atonement in the faith of the ancient prophets, it is instructive to ask two questions. First, what are the things hoped for by the prophet? Second, what is the evidence not seen? I have selected two events that illustrate Abraham's hopes, the evidence not seen, the importance of Christ in Abraham's life, and the power of his faith.

A Promised Land

The first event is described in Hebrews 11:8–10. In these verses Paul discusses the Lord's instructions to Abraham to leave his homeland and journey to a new land that would be given to him as an everlasting possession. The Lord called it a "strange" land, one unfamiliar to Abraham. Although not familiar with the route or certain of his destination, Abraham took Sarah and other family members and departed. Not only did Abraham's faith sustain him on the journey, but Paul states that it was faith that gave Abraham the courage to stay in the strange country. Paul also states that Abraham's faith caused him to look beyond Canaan "for a city . . . whose builder and maker is God" (Hebrews 11:10).

What were Abraham's hopes? The first was for a land of promise, or Canaan. The second was to be worthy of "*the* land of promise," or the heavenly city (see Hebrews 11:9). What was the evidence not seen? First, Abraham had never seen Canaan. Second, to enter the city whose builder and maker is God requires the Savior's atonement. Abraham lived 2,000 years before Christ. The Atonement had not yet occurred. He could only anticipate the Lord's sacrifice through eyes of faith.

In leading the pioneer exodus from Winter Quarters to Utah, how similar Brigham Young's hopes were to those of Abraham. He, too, sought a promised land in which the Saints could worship God and be safe from their enemies. He had never seen the Great Salt Lake Valley except through an eye of faith. When he finally reached the summit and looked down into the valley, he knew that it was the right place. However, the Saints' hopes included more than a safe haven. They, like Abraham, were looking for "*the* land of promise"—the heavenly city. Living almost 2,000 years after Christ, though the Atonement was an accomplished fact, they also had to accept that redeeming act through eyes of faith.

A Promised Son

The second event described by Paul concerns the Lord's promise to Abraham and Sarah that they would have a covenant son even though Abraham was ninety-nine and she was ninety. Hebrews 11:11–12 indicates that Sarah and Abraham received strength through faith to conceive Isaac—their son of promise. Again, what were the things hoped for? Childless to that point,

Abraham and Sarah desired a son so that their posterity might be as numerous as the sands of the seashore and the nations of the earth might be blessed through their seed. They also hoped for *The Son of Promise,* as Isaac was a type for Christ. Paul states in verse 13 that Abraham, Sarah, Isaac, and others "died in faith, not having received the promises, but having seen them afar off." Through eyes of faith they knew Jehovah would come to earth, take up a physical body, suffer in the garden, die on the cross, and be lifted up the third day. The fulfillment of Abraham's promised blessings was dependent on *The Son of Promise* as well as on *a son of promise.*

What was the evidence not yet seen? First, no woman past bearing age had ever conceived. Even Abraham's body appeared dead as to procreative power (see Genesis 18:11–12, Romans 4:19). And second, only through the eyes of faith could Christ's miraculous birth be seen or believed.

How Abraham's and Sarah's faith must have been strengthened by Isaac's miraculous birth! This was the son who would preserve the Lord's promises to the ancient patriarch. Isaac's birth must also have deepened his parents' faith in the future birth of God's Only Begotten Son. After all, the most important promise to all of us was given in the Grand Council before the creation of the earth, when the Father promised to send His Firstborn Son, who would sacrifice His life that we might live forever (see Abraham 3:22–27).

A Faith Centered in Christ

Paul's discussion of the events in Abraham's life poignantly reflects the ancient patriarch's belief in Christ. The Lord's command to Abraham to sacrifice "his only begotten son" as a type for the Savior's sacrifice highlights the focus of Abraham's faith (see Hebrews 11:17). Otherwise, how could the promise of a righteous posterity through Isaac come to pass? Paul states that Abraham believed that Isaac would be raised from the dead just as Christ would rise from His grave (see Hebrews 11:19). Abraham's knowledge of the gospel and the Savior's mission was profound. His and Isaac's trust in the Savior and the events that would transpire almost two millennia in the future carried them from Hebron to Mount Moriah believing that Isaac would be sacrificed. What sweeping joy and relief they must have felt when the angel prevented them from doing what they were prepared but so reluctant to do.

We Can Trust Him

In closing, I wish to illustrate with a modern-day story the trust that we may place in the Savior. I know that faith in Christ and obedience to the principles of the restored gospel brings answers to prayers and divine help when the hour is darkest. The story that follows concerns a young girl, the fourth child in a family of six children. Her name is Heather. Three of the children, including Heather, suffer from a rare disease called glutaric acidemia. In each case, the onset of the disease occurred during the first year of life when an enzyme attacked the brain, causing paralysis. The disease results in acid forming in the muscles, similar to that which occurs following a period of intense physical activity. The problem faced by the children is that the acid never leaves and causes great pain. Cindy, the first child with the disease, died just over one year ago at the age of twenty-three. She was one of the oldest living persons known with the disease. At death she weighed about forty pounds.

Soon after Heather's birth, her parents realized that she would be physically handicapped and that her spirit would be housed in a body with great restrictions. As she grew, she was confined to a wheelchair, unable to speak, and could only send messages with her eyes. A direct gaze and a smile meant yes. A blink meant no. Despite the physical handicaps, one could feel Heather's vibrant internal spirit.

As Heather progressed, it became obvious to the parents that she was extraordinarily bright. She would play guessing games with the family, using her limited means to communicate. When she was old enough, her parents enrolled Heather in a special school to see if she could learn to speak. The teacher was a gifted therapist. One morning as Heather and the teacher visited about the prior weekend, the teacher learned that Heather had attended Primary. The teacher then sang for Heather "When He Comes Again."[3] The expression on Heather's face revealed the delight within her. When the teacher asked Heather if she had a favorite song, the young girl's wide eyes and engaging smile left little doubt. But what was the song? Through a series of questions, the teacher learned that Heather's favorite song was one she had heard in Primary. She wasn't sure which songbook it was in, but it was about Jesus. The teacher sang all the songs she could think of, but to no avail. However, Heather was not about to quit—she wanted to share her favorite song. At the end of the day, the two were still searching. The teacher agreed to bring her Primary songbooks to school the next day.

On the following morning, Heather and her teacher continued the quest. From the first hymn to the last, the little girl blinked her eyes indicating no. They were still unsuccessful. But Heather was not about to give up. She wanted to share her favorite song. Finally, the teacher told Heather that her mother would have to help her find the song and then they would sing it. The next day Heather arrived with the green Church hymnal tucked in her wheelchair, but there was no marker. So they began with the first hymn. The teacher would sing the first part of each song and Heather would respond. To each of the first one hundred hymns, there were one hundred no's. After two hundred hymns there had been two hundred no's. Finally, the teacher began to sing "There is sunshine in my soul today . . ."[4] Heather's body jumped, and a big smile crossed her face. Her eyes gazed directly into the teacher's, indicating success after three days of searching. Both teacher and student rejoiced.

As the teacher sang the first verse and began the chorus, Heather mustered all her strength and joined in with a few sounds. After finishing the first verse and chorus, the teacher asked if she wanted to hear the rest of the verses, and Heather's eyes opened wide with a firm yes. The teacher began to sing:

> There is music in my soul today,
> A carol to my King,
> And Jesus listening can hear
> The songs I cannot sing.
> (*Hymns,* no. 227)

Heather's reaction to these lines was so strong that the teacher stopped. As the reality and significance of the words pressed on the teacher's mind, she wondered if those lines were the reason Heather so liked the song? The teacher asked: "Heather, is that what you like about the song? Is that what you want me to know? Does Jesus listen? Does He hear the songs you cannot sing?"

The direct, penetrating gaze was a clear answer.

Feeling guided by the Spirit, the teacher asked, "Heather, does Jesus talk to you in your mind and in your heart?"

Again, the child's look was penetrating.

The teacher then asked, "Heather, what does He say?"

The teacher's heart pounded as she saw the clear look in Heather's eyes as the little girl awaited the questions that would allow her to share her insights.

"Does Jesus say, 'Heather, I love you'?"

Heather's radiant eyes widened and she smiled.

After a pause, the teacher asked next, "Does He say, 'Heather, you're special'?"

The answer again was yes.

Finally, the teacher asked, "Does He say, 'Heather, be patient; I have great things in store for you'?"

With all her strength, Heather's head became erect and her eyes penetrated the teacher's soul. Heather knew she was loved, she was special, and she only needed to be patient.[5]

Two years later, Heather died because of the ravages of the disease. Her younger brother, Mark, also suffers from the disease but not to the extent of his older sisters. He can talk, although it is not easy. As the parents discussed Heather's passing and the funeral that would take place, Mark exclaimed, "No go Heather's funeral!" Heather was his best friend. As the parents tried to explain death to him, he would not be consoled or persuaded. He was crushed and did not want to attend the service. For two days he resisted.

On the morning of the funeral, the father went to Mark's room to get him up. As he entered the room, Mark was sitting up in bed with a big smile on his face. His first words were: "Dad, go Heather's funeral!"

The father responded: "Mark, what has changed your mind?"

"Dad, had dream."

"What did you dream about, Mark?"

"Dad, dreamed about Heather."

"Mark, what was Heather doing?"

"Oh, Dad, Heather running and jumping and singing 'There is sunshine in my soul today.' Dad, go Heather's funeral."[6]

I ask each of you: Would the God of this earth who learned about Heather's pains and sufferings in the garden listen to a little girl sing songs to Him even though she could not speak? Would He tell her He loves her? Would He tell her to be patient, that He has great things in store for her? If a little boy did not understand death, would He give him a dream to help him understand that life does not end with death? As Alma teaches us, Christ experienced our pains and sufferings so that He would know how to succor us (see Alma 7:11–12). We can trust Him. He earned our trust in the garden and on the cross. If we exercise faith in Him, He will respond. He will strengthen and preserve us in our time of need. May the Lord bless each of us as we develop faith in Him.

NOTES

1. Richard G. Scott, "Trust in the Lord," *Ensign* 25 (November 1995): 16–18.

2. Scott, "Trust in the Lord," 17.

3. "When He Comes Again," in *Children's Songbook of The Church of Jesus Christ of Latter-day Saints* (Salt Lake City: The Church of Jesus Christ of Latter-day Saints, 1989), 82–83.

4. "There Is Sunshine in My Soul Today," in *Hymns of The Church of Jesus Christ of Latter-day Saints* (Salt Lake City: The Church of Jesus Christ of Latter-day Saints, 1985), no. 227.

5. Story adapted from Jean Ernstrom, "Jesus, Listening, Can Hear," *Ensign* 18 (June 1988): 46–47.

6. Mark's part of the story was obtained through conversations with the parents and also from the book written by the family: Bruce and Joyce Erickson, *When Life Doesn't Seem Fair* (Salt Lake City: Bookcraft, 1995), 65–66.

CHAPTER 7

Blessings of a Testimony

(5 JANUARY 1999)

I ONCE SPOKE with a recent Brigham Young University graduate in New York City. During the conversation I detected a slight accent. I asked the young man if he was from another country. He said his homeland was Brazil, where he had spent the first twenty-three years of his life. Since few foreign converts are financially able or academically prepared to attend the university, I asked if he was a second- or third-generation member.

"No!" he responded. "I was a convert at age seventeen."

I then asked, "How much education did you have at the time of your conversion?"

His answer, "I had completed the eighth grade."

I was even more surprised. "How did you make it to BYU?" I inquired. "What motivated you to move forward with your education?"

In essence he responded, "The truths of the gospel and a mission experience convinced me of the importance of further study. Before my mission I learned about the principles of eternal progress. During the mission I had the opportunity to teach these principles to others. As I rubbed shoulders with other missionaries who had high educational aspirations, I became convinced of my own potential. When I returned from the mission field, I was determined to complete high school and move on to college. I earned a high school diploma within two years while working and saving and then applied for admission to Brigham Young University. I was accepted. I have finished a bachelor's degree and an MBA and now have excellent employment with a large multi-national corporation that utilizes my talents in both the United States and Brazil."

Simple but profound truths that we often take for granted had an enormous impact on the young Brazilian's life. He took to heart the dictum to seek "out of the best books words of wisdom; seek learning, even by study and also by faith" (D&C 88:118). He believed the revelations that state: "It is impossible for a man to be saved in ignorance" (D&C 131:6); that "the glory of God is intelligence" (D&C 93:36); that "whatever principle of intelligence we attain unto in this life, it will rise with us in the resurrection. And if a person gains more knowledge and intelligence in this life through his diligence and obedience than another, he will have so much the advantage in the world to come" (D&C 130:18–19).

Since that conversation, I have reflected again and again on the blessings of a testimony, of receiving "truth in the inward parts" (Psalm 51:6). In general we are aware of the eternal consequences of having gospel principles burned in our souls by the power of the Holy Ghost. The redemption of the soul and the inseparable connection of body and spirit coupled with eternal glory come to mind. These are of ultimate importance. But there are also more immediate blessings that flow from a testimony like that enjoyed by the young Brazilian. Not only was his eternal path changed forever, but so was his life in mortality. The motivation to improve his personal circumstances was a direct consequence of his conversion and faith. This motivation caused him to obtain an education that led to employment well beyond anything he had dreamed of as a teenager in Brazil.

The motivation to improve one's lot in life is not the only earthly consequence of conversion. There are many temporal blessings that flow from a testimony of the gospel of Jesus Christ. These include protection from the swirling winds of immorality, alcohol, tobacco, and drugs; a comfort and peace of mind that results from knowing one is not alone; a power to bless others and lighten their loads; the courage and strength to face adversity; an ability to cope with death given a knowledge of its purpose and nature.

My list is not exhaustive. I suggest you ponder the blessings of a testimony with respect to your life. See if you can add to the list. I will discuss three blessings, in addition to gaining an education.

The first is protection from the whirlwinds of the adversary; the second is the companionship of good friends; and the third concerns the courage and strength to face adversity.

Protection from the Whirlwinds of the Adversary

After many years of missionary work, Ammon spoke to his brothers about their successful labors and how their sheaves or converts needed to be gathered into garners in order for them not to be wasted. Looking forward to our time, he further stated that those gathered in the garner would "not be beaten down by the storm at the last day; yea, neither shall they be harrowed up by the whirlwinds; but when the storm cometh they shall be gathered together in their place, that the storm cannot penetrate to them; yea, neither shall they be driven with fierce winds whithersoever the enemy listeth to carry them" (Alma 26:6).

My grandfather was a farmer. I remember the garner or granary on his farm. After the exhausting task of harvesting the grain, the grain was transported to the granary for storage. The purpose of the granary was to provide a safe haven for the harvest, to protect the wheat and corn from the coming winter storms and the rain and snow that could destroy it. In addition, the garner provided protection from predators who desired the harvest for their own purposes. As the grain entered the garner, it was checked for contaminants. It was also fumigated or cleansed as a precaution and certified as to its cleanliness.

Elder Neal A. Maxwell has stated that the temple is a garner for Church members.[1] It is a place of refuge from the storms of life. He has pointed out how important it is for new converts to progress to the temple in order to be preserved. Through temple covenants members are endowed with power to protect themselves from the evil that swirls about them. Like the grain entering the garner, those entering the temple have been cleansed of contaminants through repentance, baptism, and the Holy Spirit. Moreover, they have been certified as being clean and worthy of entrance.

Brigham Young University is also one of the Lord's garners. So, too, are BYU–Hawaii, BYU–Idaho, the LDS Business College, and the seminaries and institutes spread across the earth. Each is an important gathering place for young members of the Church as a refuge from the storm. The protection provided is both temporal and spiritual. These institutions of higher learning are among the Lord's most important garners because the sheaves gathered into it are relatively young and tender. Students are at a critical stage in life. Many are on their own for the first time. Most students will make three or four of life's most important decisions while enrolled in such schools. These include the quality and type of education, a mission, marriage, and employment.

A key temporal as well as eternal blessing provided by the university is a first-class education in a moral environment. In Elder Jeffrey R. Holland's terms, the "modern winds of immorality swirl luridly around" us.[2] These winds blow through every level of society. BYU is an oasis from the storm because almost all who enter these halls of learning have a testimony of the sacredness of the human body, knowing that one's body and spirit have been purchased with a price and that life-giving processes are reserved for marriage. Individuals without testimonies, whether at other universities or in the world generally, often do not understand the severe temporal consequences of immoral acts. They do not understand that the lack of sexual discipline is one of the greatest causes of unhappiness on this earth. Families are destroyed by it or never formed because of it. Children are deprived as a result of it. How grateful we should be to associate with so many faculty, staff, and students who understand these fundamental truths and live accordingly.

Some universities are struggling with binge drinking. University officials in many parts of the nation are worried about alcohol-related deaths among students. A few administrators have taken steps to eliminate alcohol from their campuses. Alcohol not only takes lives but also interferes with the learning process. For those students with a testimony of the restored gospel, alcohol is not a problem. And those enrolled in Church-sponsored schools largely escape the destructive consequences associated with alcohol, tobacco, and drugs. Like a stake of Zion, these institutions provide "a defense, and . . . a refuge from the storm" (D&C 115:6).

One of the more obvious temporal advantages associated with living the Word of Wisdom is a healthier, longer life. A University of California at Los Angeles (UCLA) study has shown that LDS Church members live about ten years longer than their U. S. counterparts. The UCLA report indicates that Mormon high priests who never smoked cigarettes and who engage in regular physical activity have "some of the lowest mortality rates ever reported from cancer and cardiovascular disease for any population group."[3] The Word of Wisdom (D&C 89) must be a frustration to Lucifer, whose objective is to shorten life or, at a minimum, to make life miserable. The revelation, received in February 1833, has stood the test of time and is a remarkable witness of the temporal and spiritual blessings offered to the Saints. The revelation promises health, wisdom, knowledge, and the ability to "run and not be weary, and . . . walk and not faint" (D&C 89:18–20). The UCLA study provides clear evidence of the fulfillment of the promise.

The Companionship of Good Friends

Another major benefit of a testimony is the companionship of good friends. This advantage exists for Church members in general. While serving as president of the Asia North Area a few years ago, I met a recent convert whose conversion story helped me understand how a testimony builds trust among the members and allows strong friendships to be formed.

The young Japanese man was not a Christian prior to meeting the missionaries. His interest in the message was modest, but he continued to study because he enjoyed the association with the missionaries. The major stumbling block for him was a feeling of self-sufficiency; he did not understand or feel the need for a Savior. After receiving the lessons, the seed did not swell within him because he had not paid the price to receive a personal witness. The missionaries were perplexed and wondered what they should do. One day they showed him a film called *The Bridge.*[4] The film illustrates the power of Christ's atonement as a father is forced to choose between saving his son's life or the lives of passengers on a train. The film clearly underscores the dependence of the passengers on the father's decision. The young man's thoughts were provoked, and he could not sleep that night—but still there was no witness.

The next morning he went to the optician shop where he served customers needing eyeglasses. During the day an elderly woman entered. Her glasses were broken. He remembered her coming in before, but she had not had sufficient money to purchase new glasses. On this day she again showed him her broken spectacles and asked if the money she now had was sufficient. It was apparent that she was still short of funds. Then a thought came to him: "I have some money. I can make up the difference." He told her that her money was enough, took the broken spectacles, and made an appointment for her return.

When she returned a few days later, the glasses were ready. He handed them to her and she put them on.

"Miemasu! Miemasu!" [I see! I see!] Tears streamed down her cheeks in gratitude for her sight.

At that point a burning sensation was felt deep within Manabu's soul as he was encompassed by the Holy Spirit. As the woman left, he exclaimed, "Wakarimasu! Wakarimasu!" [I understand! I understand!]

His eyes and heart were opened as he felt the Savior's love and it was revealed to him that there is Someone greater than himself.

This spiritually defining moment caused a paradigm shift in the young man's life. He now knew the gospel was true. His trust in the missionaries and Church members soared. No longer was he just a receiver. Following his baptism he would stay after church meetings to meet with investigators and share his feelings and insights. He became a nurturer and a strong witness of the truth. Reaching out to others became a natural instinct. Never again would he be alone. Not only did he enjoy the companionship of the Holy Spirit, but his friendships with others in and out of the Church multiplied.

That is the blessing of our membership in the Church. Members enjoy a bond borne of mutual trust and a common interest. As Latter-day Saints, we are "children of the covenant" (3 Nephi 20:26); we have agreed through baptism to "bear one another's burdens, that they may be light; . . . mourn with those that mourn; . . . and comfort those that stand in need of comfort" (Mosiah 18:8–9). One of the great blessings emanating from Church membership is the enduring friendships we find among our brothers and sisters in the gospel.

The Courage and Strength to Face Adversity

Another of the great blessings of a testimony is the hope that comes from a knowledge of and belief in the plan of salvation. The plan provides an eternal perspective that helps the believer cope with day-to-day trials. Job's expression of hope derived from his testimony is a classic:

"For I know that my redeemer liveth, and that he shall stand at the latter day upon the earth:

"And though after my skin worms destroy this body, yet in my flesh shall I see God:

"Whom I shall see for myself, and mine eyes shall behold, and not another; though my reins be consumed within me" (Job 19:25–27).

Job was able to withstand the adversity thrust upon him by Satan: poor health, loss of family and friends, and loss of material possessions. In spite of the hardships that befell him, he was true to the end because of his strong personal witness that he was a son of God, that God had a plan for him, and that his faithfulness in the face of adversity would result in salvation.

I knew a woman whose life paralleled Job's. Her name was Joan Kinder. She was a deeply religious woman with a quick wit, a bright mind, and an engaging personality. Children and adults loved her, and she loved them. She was one of the most cheerful persons I have known. I had the privilege of teaching her the gospel when I served as a British missionary in the mid-1950s.

A decade earlier, at age twenty, she had fallen in love and was engaged to be married. It was the mid-1940s, and World War II was still raging in Europe. Her fiancé was drafted into the British army and sent to the front. She became employed in a munitions factory and waited for his return. Near the close of the war the young man's family received a letter telling of his death.

For a period of time Joan was at a loss. She joined the British equivalent of our Women's Army Corps and was sent to the Far East. In Hong Kong she met another British soldier. They fell in love and were married. Eventually they returned to England and found a home to rent in her native town. He was posted a few miles away. It was not long before they were blessed with a son.

Two years later the husband was assigned to another post some distance from their home. It was decided that she would wait for him to be established before moving to the new area. A few months went by with him returning each weekend. Each time he would suggest they wait just a little longer before making the move. Then one weekend he failed to return. She visited his base the next week. He told her that an assignment had kept him. She was uneasy, feeling that something was happening to their marriage. Within a few weeks he told her about another woman and that he wanted a divorce. She was devastated. Her son was now three years old and would grow up without a father.

It was during this time that the missionaries knocked on her door. She invited them in, accepted a Book of Mormon, and promised to read it. Within a few days she completed reading the book. A special spirit accompanied the reading and, while praying about the predicament and challenges that confronted her, a feeling of peace came along with a witness of the sacred nature of the book. The missionaries were surprised upon their return to find a convert. But she insisted on waiting a few months before joining the Church. She felt time was needed to see if her husband would change his mind. More than anything, she hoped to save her family. Time passed, and the divorce became final. She then joined the Church.

From the beginning of her membership, she was a full-tithe payer in spite of the meager income available to support her son and herself. She worked in a small shop where her boy could be with her until he entered school. Then she became a seamstress in a factory with better pay. Her leadership abilities eventually resulted in her becoming part of the management staff. When her son was grown, she immigrated to this country and found employment with the Family History Department of the Church. She was a specialist in reading old English and old German manuscripts.

One day she received a call from the British Embassy in Washington, D. C. They asked for a meeting and sent a representative to see her. She was told in the meeting that her son had been killed while on business in a foreign country. For a period of time there was a sadness in her eyes and a heaviness in her heart. Then the cheerfulness returned. The twinkle in her eyes, her quick wit, and her love for people were irrepressible. My children loved to be in her presence. There was something special about this deeply faithful woman.

Not many years after her son's death, Joan was crossing a street in Salt Lake City on her way to work. The morning sun had just topped the mountains in the east, and a woman driving east failed to see Joan in the crosswalk. Apparently Joan was not aware of the car coming at her. Suddenly there was an impact. The car hit her with tremendous force. Her time in mortality was over. A short time later I received a call from a mutual friend informing me of the accident and her death.

I have thought often about this wonderful, interesting woman. Her life was filled with tragedy. Most of the things she wanted in life never materialized. One did—the greatest one! She found the hope that comes with a testimony of the gospel. In the end, that satisfied her. She knew she would see her son again. Parents and friends were eternal. She found joy in the gospel here and knew that unspeakable joy would be hers on the other side of the veil.

May we appreciate the wonderful blessings available to us in this life through the gospel of Jesus Christ. May our testimonies motivate us to improve our lot in life, to withstand the temptations of the adversary, to enjoy good friends, and to face adversity with hope and courage, knowing that joy awaits us in the eternities.

NOTES

1. See Neal A. Maxwell, "Coordination of Full-Time and Stake Missionary Work," (paper presented at the Regional Representative Seminar, 30 March 1990), 6.

2. Jeffrey R. Holland, "Personal Purity," *Ensign* 28 (November 1998): 75.

3. Vicki Beck, "UCLA School of Public Health Study Finds Mormon Health Practices Linked to Unusually Low Rate of Cancer and Cardiovascular Deaths," *UCLA News,* 5 December 1989; see also James E. Enstrom, "Health Practices and Cancer Mortality Among Active California Mormons," *Journal of the National Cancer Institute* 81, no. 23 (6 December 1989): 1807–14.

4. *The Bridge* (North Centerville, Utah: Visual Transit Authority Thomson Productions, Inc., 1987).

CHAPTER 8

Christ Is the Reason

(16 JANUARY 2001)

THIS IS AN especially important time in the history of the earth. The Church's assigned effort to take the gospel to every nation, kindred, tongue, and people is moving forward at a rapid pace. The world is being prepared for the return of its Creator. We know not the day nor the hour of His coming. Some signs still remain unfulfilled. However, key events associated with the Savior's triumphant return are being recorded on the pages of history. The gospel has been restored, Elijah has returned, missionaries are working in many countries, and temples are beginning to dot the earth. Handel's glorious anthem "Lift Up Your Heads" is a reminder of the day when the gates of the New Jerusalem, the holy city, will be open for the Savior of the world and all of Israel to enter (see Psalm 24:7; Revelation 21:21–25).

Sister Bateman and I have been reflecting on eternal truths and the principles and values that must motivate our actions if we are to qualify for entry into that holy place. We would like to

121

share some of our thoughts, based on an experience we had in Japan a few years ago.

In the summer of 1993, Sister Bateman and I received an assignment to serve in the Asia North Area, which included Japan, Korea, and far east Russia. The opportunity to live and work in that part of the world was exciting. We had lived in Europe and Africa earlier, but Asia was new to us. As a member of the area presidency, I had responsibility for the stakes, districts, and missions in the three countries. One of the key assignments was to conduct mission tours. Each mission of the Church is visited annually by a General Authority, usually a member of the area presidency. The presidency member and his wife travel with the mission president and his wife throughout the mission, observing the work and visiting with and interviewing missionaries.

Shortly after our arrival in Japan, a mission tour was scheduled for the Fukuoka Mission on the island of Kyushu. Sister Bateman and I were to meet with President and Sister Cyril Figuerres and tour the mission. A few days before the tour began, a tropical storm, one of the worst in the history of Japan, struck Kyushu with typhoon force, wreaking havoc across the island. The city of Kagoshima on the island's southern tip was particularly hard hit as roofs were ripped off buildings, homes were demolished as they slid down mountainsides, trains came to a halt, and cars were swept into the ocean. Initially, there was concern about the safety and welfare of the missionaries and Saints, but reports confirmed that everyone was safe.

A few days later we learned of many acts of service that the missionaries had rendered during the storm. Missionaries had directed traffic at busy intersections where stoplights had failed. Two missionaries had helped a man change a flat tire in the midst of the gale as the owner was unable to secure his car on the jack and remove the spare tire from the trunk. Throughout the island missionaries had assisted people in protecting their homes and personal belongings. Over and over the missionaries demonstrated love for the people through acts of kindness and service. In the week immediately following the storm, missionaries spent hours and days helping to clean homes of thick layers of mud and assisting with repairs.

Approximately one week after the storm, Sister Bateman and I met President and Sister Figuerres in Fukuoka on the north end of the island and then flew to Kagoshima to begin the mission tour. We drove from the airport to the chapel where the missionaries were waiting to begin a zone conference. As we entered the parking lot, we noticed the missionaries standing outside the chapel in a line waiting to greet us. I remember that as we got out of the car and approached the missionaries, the Spirit was so strong that it brought tears to our eyes and we could hardly contain our feelings. Their countenances exuded light. They were clean and well dressed, and their mannerisms reflected an inner peace and humility. A strong impression came that they had had an extraordinary experience—a refining one—as they had become Ammon-like servants to the Japanese people and to the Master. The discussions that ensued in the zone conference, the lessons taught, and the testimonies borne confirmed our impressions.

After the conference Sister Bateman and I discussed what we had seen and felt. We wondered if the experiences associated with the storm were primarily responsible for the special spirit that prevailed among the Kagoshima missionaries. Obviously they had been impacted by the events. But as we continued the tour and observed missionaries in other parts of the mission, we found a similar pattern of faith, obedience, and motivation to serve. We eventually concluded that there were a number of reasons for the faith and power displayed by the missionaries: the mission president was an effective teacher; the missionaries were obedient and responded to his teachings; and, like Ammon and the other sons of Mosiah, they studied the scriptures, they fasted and prayed, they worked hard, and they "taught with power and authority" (see Alma 17:2–3).

As we observed, Sister Bateman and I came to understand that the lives of these young men and women had been impacted by a mission motto developed by the president, which the missionaries had accepted as a guide. The principles embodied in that motto apply not only to missionary activity but to everyday life. The motto reads:

> Faith is the power,
> Obedience is the price,
> Love is the motive,
> The Spirit is the key, and
> Christ is the reason.[1]

Sister Bateman and I will take turns discussing these principles. Sister Bateman will begin, discussing the roles of faith and love in our lives; and I will conclude with remarks concerning obedience, the Spirit as the key, and "Christ Is the Reason."

Faith Is the Power (Sister Bateman)

Why is faith included in the mission motto? What is faith? Faith is a confidence and a trust in something. In Hebrews 11:1 we read, "Now faith is the substance [confidence or assurance] of things hoped for, the evidence [or proof] of things not seen."

Faith is a principle of power. It is active. It causes things to happen. Some equate faith with belief. But faith is more dynamic

CHRIST IS THE REASON

than belief. Compared with faith, belief is passive. Belief is just an acceptance that something is so. For instance, even the devils believe in Christ, but they don't trust Him or follow Him (see Mark 1:23–24; 5:1–18).

The scriptures state (specifically, Alma 32:21 and Hebrews 11:1) that faith is not a perfect knowledge but a hope or evidence of something not seen that is true. The Prophet Joseph Smith taught that faith motivates our day-to-day activities, that faith "is the moving cause of all action."[2] Because faith dwells within the heart of every person on this earth, we are constantly using this power in sowing seeds of one kind or another with the assurance that sooner or later we will reap a harvest. For instance, the farmer plants seeds in his field with the hope of a harvest. Scholars and students exert themselves in pursuit of an education—and eventually graduation—because they *believe* they can obtain their goal. The same thing is true with missionary efforts. If new missionaries feel they can find a golden contact and then put forth much effort, they will be successful. No wonder faith was an important principle of the Fukuoka Mission motto. Missionaries must have faith in themselves. They must have faith in the message they are teaching. They must have faith in the Lord.

Without such faith, the Prophet Joseph said, "Both mind and body would be in a state of inactivity, and all their exertions would cease, both physical and mental."[3] If a missionary sat around and did nothing, President Figuerres, the mission president, knew that this missionary needed an increase of faith. "As faith is the moving cause of all action in temporal concerns," the Prophet continued, "so it is in spiritual [things]."[4] All blessings, temporal and spiritual, we receive through faith.

Having faith in ourselves is an important ingredient in accomplishing our goals. We want to graduate from college, so we exert every effort to make it happen. However, some people put all their faith in themselves. Faith in ourselves can be motivating, but it is not saving—and by itself it cannot be sustained. It does not lead to life and salvation. Saving faith centers in the Lord Jesus Christ and through Him in the Father. The Apostle Paul preached that "there is none other name under heaven given among men, whereby we must be saved" (Acts 4:12). Jacob taught that men must have "perfect faith in the Holy One of Israel [Jesus Christ], or they cannot be saved in the kingdom of God" (2 Nephi 9:23).

Faith in the Lord Jesus Christ is the first principle of the gospel. Faith in Him is more than acknowledgment that He lives. It is more than professing belief. Faith in the Savior consists of sure and complete reliance on Him. As God, He has infinite power, intelligence, and love. There is no human problem beyond His ability to solve. He descended below all things. He knows how to succor His people according to their needs. We must have "unshaken faith in him, relying wholly upon the merits of him who is mighty to save" (2 Nephi 31:19). Faith in Him means that even though we do not understand all things, we know that He does. We must look to Him "in every thought; doubt not, fear not" (D&C 6:36).

The gospel of Jesus Christ is the perfect prescription for all human problems and social ills. But His gospel is effective only as it is applied in our lives. To show our desire to be one with our Savior, to show our gratitude for the great mercy that He has extended to us, to help us gain eternal life, we must be actively engaged in showing forth our faith. We do this by prayer, scripture study, keeping the commandments, attending church, giving service to others, and fulfilling our callings and duties in the Church. We do it by expressing our testimony of Him, the Son of God.

There was a strong faith in Peter's mind and heart when the

Lord asked: "Whom say ye that I am? And Simon Peter answered and said, Thou art the Christ, the Son of the living God" (Matthew 16:15–16).

Nor was there any wavering in Peter when Christ taught the multitude at Capernaum, declaring Himself to be the bread of life. Many of those there would not accept His teachings and "went back, and walked no more with him. Then said Jesus unto the twelve, Will ye also go away? Then Simon Peter answered him, Lord, to whom shall we go? thou hast the words of eternal life. And we believe and are sure that thou art that Christ, the Son of the living God" (John 6:66–69).

Christ is the Son of the living God, and He does indeed have the words of eternal life.

Love Is the Motive (Sister Bateman)

"Love is the motive" is a powerful principle in the Fukuoka Mission motto. As President Figuerres urged the missionaries to be obedient and develop their faith, he also encouraged them to mature to the point where their actions and goals were not motivated by fear or reward or duty but by a love for the Lord and for those they served. The highest motive for keeping the commandments is a love for God and for His children. In fact, Christ has told us that the two great commandments—to love the Lord and to love our neighbors—are the foundation for every other commandment (see Matthew 22:36–40).

Love is a gift. It is difficult for us to love others if we are not loved. Sometimes we don't feel loved or at all lovable. At these times it may be difficult for us to feel motivated to exercise faith or to show love. But God loves us. He loves us more than we can comprehend at this time. We need to come to understand how great His love is: "For God so loved the world, that he gave his only begotten Son, that whosoever believeth in him should not perish, but have everlasting life" (John 3:16). Many converts to the Church report the overwhelming joy they feel in being converted to the gospel of Jesus Christ. They feel God's love for them, and it is this love that entices them to be baptized and follow Him. John reminded us, "We love him, because he first loved us" (1 John 4:19). I, too, have felt this love, a burning love that encompasses my whole soul. When it is in you, it enlightens you, *all of you,* and transforms you.

One way we can experience a greater confirmation of God's love is through keeping our hearts and minds pure. Jacob exhorted: "Look unto God with firmness of mind, and pray unto him with exceeding faith, and he will console you in your afflictions, and he will plead your cause. . . . O all ye that are pure in heart, lift up your heads and receive the pleasing word of God, and feast upon his love; for ye may, if your minds are firm, forever" (Jacob 3:1–2).

Fasting and prayer can bring us closer to the Lord and rekindle in us the fire of love that brought us to commit ourselves to the Savior in the first place. We have been promised that if we keep the Lord's commandments with a sincere desire to do what is right, He will not withhold His love from us:

"As the Father hath loved me, so have I loved you: continue ye in my love.

"If ye keep my commandments, ye shall abide in my love; even as I have kept my Father's commandments, and abide in his love.

"These things have I spoken unto you, that my joy might remain in you, and that your joy might be full.

"This is my commandment, That ye love one another, as I have loved you" (John 15:9–12).

We need to have faith that the Lord does indeed love us. As we exercise that faith through obedience, we begin to feel the Lord's love more powerfully in our lives. All of these principles are interconnected; they engender and reinforce each other. As we feel the Lord's love take root in our hearts, as we taste of that sweetest of all fruits, then our love is kindled for those around us.

There are so many of our Father's children in the world today who need our love, who need us to reach out and bring them into our circle. It may be that your expression of love provides the spark that witnesses to them that God loves them. Through your loving actions they may gain an assurance that God is a loving God in whom they can place their faith. I am touched by the chorus of a song by Deanna Edwards entitled "Am I Beautiful to You?"

> Am I beautiful to you?
> Have you eyes to see my soul?
> Do you know that I'm a child of God
> And your love can make me whole?
> Am I beautiful to you?
> Do you see my light within?
> Please love me from the inside out—
> Not from the outside in.[8]

Share your own rich stores of love with those around you. You will find that as you do, you will only continue to reap more love and joy.

Our obedience takes on new meaning as we cross over from keeping the letter of the law and begin to keep the spirit of the law. Obedience, faith, and love are not easily separated from each other. The source of our faith comes from understanding the nature of God—that He is a good and loving God who has the power to save us. The source of our obedience rests in a love for God and in the faith that by keeping the commandments we will partake more fully of God's love. It is my hope that each of us will exercise the faith necessary to call upon the Lord and receive a witness that He lives and that He loves us. It is my prayer that with this renewed confirmation of God's love we may open our hearts to others.

Obedience Is the Price (President Bateman)

President Figuerres told us his desire was to teach his missionaries the importance of being obedient to gospel principles, knowing they would then govern themselves properly. He knew that missionaries would obey missionary rules if they believed in and were committed to a higher set of principles. Thus he spent minimal time teaching rules from the missionary handbook but considerable time teaching from the scriptures. The Savior and Ammon were the role models. The mission president infused in the missionaries a desire to be Ammon-like in their service to the Japanese people. President Figuerres believed that if the missionaries would humble themselves; repent; render quiet acts of service; and spend time studying, fasting, praying, finding, and teaching, converts would follow. His efforts were rewarded. Missionaries were obedient to the missionary handbook because they were obedient to a higher set of laws; and they found investigators to teach who then found the gospel because of the way in which these young men and women lived.

I feel the same way about students and the Honor Code at Brigham Young University. For the most part, you live the Honor Code not because you signed your name on a document but because you were taught a higher law in your homes before coming to the university. That is true for members and nonmembers alike. It is faith in a higher order that causes you to act and look the way you do. More than 90 percent of you stated in a recent national survey that you have never seen another student cheat on an exam at this university. The average for other universities is 55 percent.[5] In addition, you strive to live morally clean lives and dress modestly because you understand the sacred nature of the human body and desire to treat it as a temple. In discussing the purposes of mortality, we point to the necessity of obtaining a physical body as a housing for the spirit so that we can become like our Father in Heaven. We don't often point out, however, that it is the physical body combined with the spirit that contains god-like, creative power. And if we honor that sacred power in mortality, we will have it in eternity. If we abuse that power, we will lose it. Our success as a university stems from your obedience based on faith in the Father and the Son and in the restoration of the gospel.

To illustrate this point, visitors to campus notice almost immediately a difference between this university and others. They remark on the cleanliness, the order that exists, and the light in people's countenances. Invariably they ask why the students are so happy.

Two years ago a high government official from Europe was sitting by me at lunch. We were discussing the questions asked by the students and his tour of campus. During the conversation he said, "Last week I visited another campus in another state. The students were different from yours. If some of those students were brought to this campus, could you make them look like your students?"

I replied, "No! I don't believe so! We would have to start with their parents!"

Behavior is a function of faith, and faith is determined by one's willingness to submit, to be obedient to higher laws, to "experiment upon [the] word" (Alma 32:27). The Savior declared that the power to redeem all mankind came from the Father as a result of His willingness to be obedient. He stated: "I can of mine own self do nothing: as I hear, I judge: and my judgment is just; because I seek not mine own will, but the will of the Father which hath sent me" (John 5:30).

On another occasion Jesus said: "For I have not spoken of myself; but the Father which sent me, he gave me a commandment, what I should say, and what I should speak.

"Whatsoever I speak therefore, even as the Father said unto me, so I speak" (John 12:49–50).

Referring to the Savior's words, a BYU professor wrote the following:

> Without such obedience and unity with the Father, the Lord could not have redeemed us. How else could he have had the power to stay with his mission in the face of the awful suffering it entailed? How else, except by suffering for us, could he have come to love us the way he did? (Alma 7:11–12.)[6]

Obedience is the price that produces faith, love, access to the Holy Spirit, and, ultimately, access to the celestial kingdom. It is the first law of heaven. Sister Bateman will now discuss the second and third principles of the motto.

As President Bateman has so powerfully illustrated, obedience is the price we pay to come closer to our Heavenly Father. Obedience is a way of demonstrating our faith. Obedience confirms that our belief is more than passive, that it is an active force within us. Elder Bruce R. McConkie observed that there is a vital connection between obedience and faith. He explained: "Faith is a gift of God bestowed as a reward for personal righteousness. It is always given when righteousness is present, and the greater the measure of obedience to God's laws the greater will be the endowment of faith."[7]

There is a kind of feedback loop between obedience and faith. We obey God's will based on the measure of faith we have in us, but as we obey, the Lord strengthens our faith even more. As we continue to exercise faith through our actions, our faith grows.

The Spirit Is the Key (President Bateman)

Sister Bateman mentioned a feedback loop that exists between obedience and faith. She stated, "We obey God's will based on the measure of faith we have in us, but as we obey, the Lord strengthens our faith even more."

What is the connecting link between obedience-producing faith and then greater faith leading to more obedience? As President Figuerres noted, "the Spirit is the key." The Holy Ghost is the connecting link, the key to the relationship. The Holy Spirit confirms one's obedience to gospel principles with an assurance or witness that one is living appropriately. The confirmation or witness adds to one's knowledge, which increases faith (see Alma 32:28–30). Additional faith increases access to the Spirit, which helps us be even more obedient. The spiritual assurances may be in the form of a burning sensation, a peaceful feeling, or increased joy or love. The Holy Ghost has many fruits with which to bless a person and increase one's testimony (see Galatians 5:22–23).

The spiritual assurance through the Holy Ghost connects with the powers of the Atonement to change one's nature from that of the natural man or woman to that of a saint or celestial person. Listen to King Benjamin's words:

"For the natural man is an enemy to God, and has been from the fall of Adam, and will be, forever and ever, unless he yields to the enticings of the Holy Spirit, and putteth off the natural man and becometh a saint through the atonement of Christ the Lord, and becometh as a child, submissive, meek, humble, patient, full of love, willing to submit to all things which the Lord seeth fit to inflict upon him, even as a child doth submit to his father" (Mosiah 3:19).

The Holy Ghost serves the Father and the Son. He is our connecting link to them. Christ promised the eleven Apostles after the Last Supper that He would send another Comforter, even the Spirit of Truth (see John 14:16–17), who would "teach [them] all things, and bring all things to [their] remembrance" and "guide [them] into all truth . . . and [show them] things to come" (John 14:26; 16:13). The Savior further said that the Holy Ghost would not speak for Himself but would receive from Christ that which He was to tell and show us.

The Savior knows us perfectly. Through the Atonement He knows how to succor us (see Alma 7:11–12). When one receives a prompting in answer to a question asked in prayer or a feeling of love for another person, or if one has a confirming feeling during a person's testimony, where do those come from? One should recognize first of all that the Holy Ghost is at work. In addition, since the Holy Spirit represents the Savior, one should also recognize that the ultimate source of those feelings or those promptings is the Redeemer Himself.

Have you ever thought of the many roles played by the Holy Ghost in our lives? He is a cleanser, a guide, a teacher, a justifier, a healer, a witness, a comforter, a quickener, a revelator, a sealer, and a sanctifier. He is the key. He knows when we are obedient. He knows how to comfort us when in need. He knows how to assist us without abrogating agency.

Christ Is the Reason (President Bateman)

As members of The Church of Jesus Christ of Latter-day Saints, we are blessed through modern revelation to know more about Christ and His purposes than any other people on earth. We know him as Jehovah in the Old Testament and as the Son of God in the New Testament (see 1 Nephi 21:26; Mosiah 3:5–8; D&C 110:3–4). We know His relationship to the Father as the Firstborn spirit in premortality and as the Son of God in the flesh with Mary as His mother (see Colossians 1:15; 1 Nephi 11:18–21; D&C 110:4). We understand the Father's plan presented in the premortal council and the Savior's willingness to serve as the executor of the covenant—to be the Mediator and Redeemer of all mankind (see Abraham 3:22–26). We know our relationship to Him—He is our Eldest Brother in the spirit (see Abraham 3:27–28). These truths are not generally understood by the world.

We also have a broad understanding of His earthly mission, including the Atonement (see 2 Nephi 9; Mosiah 3:5–11; Alma 7:11–12; 34:10, 14; 3 Nephi 11:11; D&C 19:16–19). We certainly know more about the Atonement and the Lord's power to change us from mortality to immortality and from corruptible to incorruptible beings because of the teachings of the Book of Mormon and the Doctrine and Covenants (see Alma 41; D&C 76). We know about His mission to the Western Hemisphere, which is not understood by others (see 3 Nephi 11–28). We know about His work in the spirit world. We understand the Resurrection and its meaning for Him and for us (see 2 Nephi 2:8; 9:12; Alma 11:41, 45; 41:4; 3 Nephi 11; Moroni 10:34; D&C 29:26; 93:33). Finally, we know about His sealing power. We understand that a key purpose of this earth is to form eternal families and that, through the Atonement, Christ has the power to bind men and women together for eternity.

Christ is the basis for all that we do. He is the reason we do missionary work. Without the Savior and His Atonement, there would be no good news to spread. Without Him, temple work would be in vain. Our progress would stop. But He did partake of the bitter cup and "finished [His] preparations unto the children of men" (D&C 19:18–19). As we come to know Him and to "learn . . . that there is no other way or means whereby man can be saved, only in and through Christ" (Alma 38:9), we become better students, we have a stronger influence on others, we serve more faithfully as missionaries, we raise better families, and we become worthy to enter the Holy City, following the footsteps of Abraham, Isaac, and Jacob.

I will close with a story that illustrates the influence we can have on those who observe us, if we are obedient to the principles of the gospel and to the sacred commitments we have made. The story also speaks of the power that missionaries have to change peoples' lives. The moral of the story is the same whether you are a student at BYU, a missionary in Japan, or simply a member somewhere in the world.

Recently, as I discussed the Fukuoka Mission motto and the typhoon experience with President Figuerres, he shared the following story of something that happened to a member of the Church during the Kyushu storm in 1993:

Brother Mitsunori Sumiya was rushing home from work in the torrential rain. He could barely see through the windshield [of his car]. He tried earnestly to dodge debris blowing across the streets. Traffic was chaotic because traffic lights no longer functioned. He explained that everyone seemed to be looking after their own personal welfare as they hurried home.

Then he experienced a "defining moment" in his life. He saw young missionaries directing traffic at intersections. Further along he saw two missionaries helping a man change a flat tire. As he continued home he saw other missionaries assisting people in various ways. This good brother said he had a feeling of shame come over him because he realized that his constant prayer and only focus was to protect his car from being damaged. In stark contrast, the young missionaries' only focus seemed to be in serving others.

The member then received an empowering insight: "My core values are not rooted in Christ, but in worldly things like my car. These young missionaries, only half my age, have Christ-like values." He realized that it is often in times of emotional stress and anxiety that one's true values are revealed.

Months later the member said to [President Figuerres], "Your missionaries are truly modern-day Ammons who serve the people of Japan spontaneously and without being compelled. They are constantly serving everyone, all the time, and everywhere because they want to, . . . because love is their driving motive."

During the years that followed, Brother Sumiya deepened his roots in Christ as a result of that experience, and his life began to change. Brother Sumiya became the first president of the newly organized Kumamoto Stake a few years ago.[9]

It is my hope that we will enjoy the power that comes with faith, that we will not shortchange ourselves in paying the price of obedience, that we will have love as our motive, that we will live worthy to receive the Holy Spirit in our lives, and that we will know that Christ is the reason.

NOTES

1. Japan Fukuoka Mission Motto, 1991–1994.

2. N. B. Lundwall, comp., *Lectures on Faith* (Salt Lake City: Bookcraft, n.d.), 7 [1:10].

3. Lundwall, *Lectures on Faith,* 7 [1:10].

4. Lundwall, *Lectures on Faith,* 8 [1:12].

5. "Academic Integrity Study," Center for Academic Integrity, Duke University, fall 1999.

6. Allen E. Bergin, "The Way to Christlike Love," *Ensign* 12 (December 1982): 51.

7. Bruce R. McConkie, *Mormon Doctrine,* 2nd ed., rev. (Salt Lake City: Bookcraft, 1966), 264, s.v. "faith."

8. In Deanna Edwards, *Share Love's Light* (Provo, Utah: Rock Canyon Music Publishers, 1990), 27–29.

9. Cyril Figuerres to Merrill J. Bateman, 12 January 2000, copy of letter in my possession.

CHAPTER 9

Hope for Peace

(11 SEPTEMBER 2001)

T HIS MORNING, one of the greatest tragedies that has occurred on the mainland of the United States took place. Thousands of lives have been lost, and thousands have been injured. The most important counsel that we can give this morning, I believe, is threefold.

The first is there is no reason to fear for our lives or the lives of our loved ones if they weren't in those towers or the Pentagon. We suspect the terrorists are hoping for panic. With the exception again of the Pentagon and the World Trade Center, we believe there are no other areas of danger.

Second, it is extremely important that we be respectful of all people. When the Oklahoma City federal building was bombed, there was considerable speculation early on as to who might have been responsible. In the end those speculations were incorrect. We ask all of you to be respectful of every single person that you meet and contact here on campus and elsewhere.

Third, the best news of all is the good news. It is the gospel of

Jesus Christ. Even though we live in troubled times—and prophets have indicated that there will be turmoil in the last days—it is possible for each of us to feel peace, to have the peace of the gospel in our lives. We believe that is the most important message we have for the world.

We are part of the greatest peaceful mission this earth has ever known. The 60,000 missionaries and eleven million members of the Church have the only message that gives hope for peace. And peace will not come in the lives of people until they have internalized the message of the Master.

Let me turn to the words of the Savior. At the Last Supper, after finishing the meal, the Savior and His disciples sang the Hallel. The words of the Hallel are from Psalms 113 through 118. Psalms 113 through 116 are traditionally sung before the meal, in which thanks are given to God for the deliverance of the children of Israel from Egypt; Psalms 117 and 118 are sung after the Passover meal. I invite you to read those chapters in Psalms. Those chapters talk about being saved from death. They are talking about the Atonement. So, at the Last Supper with His eleven disciples—Judas having left to work his perfidy—Jesus is singing about His own death.

In that setting, in advance of the suffering and cruelty He was about to endure and the disciples' own trial of faith and courage, He told them about the most precious gift He had to give them. That gift was the gift of the Holy Ghost. These are His words: "But the Comforter, which is the Holy Ghost, whom the Father will send in my name, he shall teach you all things, and bring all things to your remembrance, whatsoever I have said unto you" (John 14:26).

And then He said, "Peace I leave with you, my peace I give unto you" (John 14:27).

He knows that death awaits, but there is peace in His heart. He knows He is going into the garden and onto the cross. And yet, He is at peace and is extending peace to His disciples.

"Peace I leave with you, my peace I give unto you: not as the world giveth, give I unto you. Let not your heart be troubled, neither let it be afraid" (John 14:27).

On this somber occasion, when our nation has been so blatantly attacked, that is the message of the gospel, the message of The Church of Jesus Christ of Latter-day Saints. Fortunately mortality is only the second act of a three-act play. Even when death comes to those we love, we know that life in the spirit is not ended. We know those who have lost their lives are fine. The curtain on the second act has closed, but an unending third act has just begun. It is those of us who are left behind who are sad. We know we will see them again, and we know we will be with them. When death comes to someone who has the peace of the Holy Ghost inside, it can be sweet, not bitter.

Do you understand why members of the Church hold the power of peace for the world in their hands? The world depends on us.

As members of the Church we know the plan of salvation. It is our duty to proclaim the Restoration, to testify of eternal life, to declare the peace the gospel brings. Whatever peace the world is capable of experiencing is on our shoulders because we have the only message that gives hope for eternal peace.

Learning in the Light of Truth

CHAPTER 10

Light, Visions, and Dreams

(19 SEPTEMBER 2000)

I WISH TO EXPRESS appreciation to Sister Bateman for the extraordinary companion she has been to me through four decades. While I have tried to fulfill my dreams, many of which pertain to a temporal setting, she has focused solely on matters of eternal consequence. Her time and energy have been given to supporting a husband, raising children, befriending neighbors, visiting those with special needs, and creating a wonderful, peaceful home. She is a quiet, self-effacing woman—one who does not seek the limelight. Her life is one of devotion to the Master. It is one of unselfishness. I cannot thank her enough. Although my words may embarrass her, I pay tribute to a remarkable friend and companion.

My thoughts are centered on the dreams and visions that inspire temporal and spiritual progress and the principles that produce growth and achievement. Scientific discoveries during the last one hundred years exceed the cumulative findings of all the centuries that preceded it. I do not believe that the increase in knowledge is happenstance. It is part of the Lord's plan as he bestows additional light upon the earth's inhabitants. The Lord told Joseph Smith that the restoration of the gospel would be but a beginning to the light that He would pour out upon the earth—not only spiritual light but also light that pertains to this temporal world (see D&C 121:26–32).

Recently, I became fascinated with the nature of light and its characteristics.[1] All of us are aware of the natural light that emanates from the sun, which provides the heat and light that sustain temporal life on earth. In contrast, few of the earth's inhabitants are aware of the spiritual light that emanates from a different Son—our "bright and morning star" (Revelation 22:16). Even fewer people appreciate the close relationship between spiritual and natural light.

Physicists have studied light for many years, fascinated by its dual nature. Photons of light behave like streams of particles in some circumstances and like waves in others. In a diffraction experiment, light appears to be a wave. When light is used to bombard certain materials, it appears to be composed of particles. The German physicist Max Planck developed a theory in the early 1900s that "helped explain how tiny particles, such as photons, behave like waves. His theory . . . helped scientists accept the idea that light behaves like both particles and waves."[2]

Another form of light not studied by physicists is light in the spiritual dimension. As members of the Church we are privileged to know about, access, and benefit from a more refined light that emanates from Christ. It, too, is the source of life—eternal life. This light, the Light of Christ, is the source of truth. In speaking to Joseph Smith, the Savior said: "For the word of the Lord is truth, and whatsoever is truth is light, and whatsoever is light is Spirit, even the Spirit of Jesus Christ. And the Spirit giveth light to every man that cometh into the world; and the Spirit enlighteneth every man through the world, that hearkeneth to the voice of the Spirit" (D&C 84:45–46).

In the study of light, physicists have discovered that light has a spectrum. The visible portion of that spectrum displays many colors. The light spectrum has proven useful as physicists and engineers have designed equipment that allows each color to be used as a conduit, thereby multiplying the carrying capacity of light.

The physical spectrum of light has a spiritual counterpart. The spiritual spectrum pertains to various levels of intelligence, beginning with animal instinct and moving to more refined forms of understanding and behavior. The higher gradations of light and truth include man's ability to reason and the operation of conscience, the light that comes through the Holy Ghost prior to baptism, and the light one receives through the gift of the Holy Ghost after entering the Lord's kingdom. Finally, a fullness of light is received when one has proven worthy of the Second Comforter and receives the "more sure word of prophecy" (2 Peter 1:19; D&C 131:5).[3]

More than one hundred years ago, President Charles W. Penrose, citing section 88 of the Doctrine and Covenants, stated that the physical and spiritual spectrums of light are related and belong to one continuum. Speaking of the Light of Christ, he said:

> It is the light and the life of all things. It is the light and the life of man. It is the life of the animal creation. It is the life of the vegetable creation. It is in the earth . . . ; it is in the stars . . . ; it is in the moon . . . : it is in the sun, and is the light of the sun, and the power by which it was made; and these grosser particles of light that illuminate

the heavens and enable us to behold the works of nature, are from that same Spirit which enlightens our minds and unfolds the things of God. As that light comes forth from the sun, so the light of God comes to us.[4]

Brigham Young University is part of the miracle of the Restoration. The goal of the university is to be filled with light and truth—both temporally and spiritually. In order for this to occur, all who are involved must be diligent and obedient in pursuing truth if we are to be conduits of the full spectrum. Brigham Young University is unique in that it is the only university that can develop curriculum in the context of the restored gospel. (The same can be said of BYU–Idaho and BYU–Hawaii.) This is our core competency. Centuries ago the Old Testament prophet Joel spoke of our day and of the events preceding the Lord's Second Coming in the following words: "And it shall come to pass . . . that I will pour out my spirit upon all flesh; and your sons and your daughters shall prophesy, your old men shall dream dreams, your young men shall see visions: . . .

"And I will shew wonders in the heavens and in the earth" (Joel 2:28, 30).

The Lord promised Joel that He would pour out His Spirit upon young people, that your generation would see visions that would light the way and provide insights to increase faith and improve life. Sometimes in thinking of visions, dreams, and revelation, we think of an epiphany—an extraordinary event like Joseph's vision in the Sacred Grove or the appearance of Moroni. Generally, however, that is not the way the Lord works with us. More often, revelation comes quietly in the form of thoughts and ideas that seem to be pure intelligence flowing into us and teaching us things we did not know. The Prophet Joseph Smith, in speaking of revelation, said: "A person may profit by noticing the first intimation of the spirit of revelation; for instance, when you feel pure intelligence flowing into you, it may give you sudden strokes of ideas, so that by noticing it, you may find it fulfilled the same day or soon."[5]

I received a letter from a young BYU student describing such an experience. A portion of the letter reads:

> Recently I sat in a physics class and had the Holy Ghost teach me. We were discussing fiber optics and how light travels perfectly through strands of [glass] without losing energy. I realized as the lecture proceeded that all things point to Christ. Christ has all power and never "loses energy" as He influences our lives. I sat in awe at the understanding that came to me; not a physical understanding but a spiritual enlightenment filled my soul. I came out of that lecture on a spiritual high.[6]

The young woman's insight is profound. As an infinite source of all power, the Savior does not lose energy as He assists us in the learning process and in our quest for eternal life. The student's connection to the Spirit and her insight illustrate the power of learning when temporal understanding combines with faith to produce a spiritual confirmation.

The prophet Joel's statement has caused me to reflect on the experiences that have changed my life, from the time I was a young man to my dreams today. Such an experience occurred in my late teens when a bishop called me to teach a Sunday School class of eight-year-olds. I will always remember the trepidation I felt prior to the first class and the wonderment that someone believed in me enough to trust young people to my stewardship. I put my heart and soul into preparing for the class. I studied the scriptures as well as the manual and enjoyed the beauty and cogency of the Lord's word. One day as I was preparing a lesson, a thought came to me regarding the importance of the Lord's teachings and the scriptures and their applicability in my life. A strong, warm sensation saturated my being as the thought passed through my consciousness. That day I felt the swellings of the Holy Spirit within me, and I sensed the power that comes when one searches the scriptures. It was the beginning of a personal testimony.

Years later, as the dean of a business school, I had another dream. It was more mundane. I remember leaving my office and entering the secretarial area. Four secretaries were at work on IBM Selectric typewriters. The noise was deafening as the keys struck the paper. If the Occupational Safety and Heath Administration had been around, a citation would have been issued. In my mind's eye I saw the day when silent typewriters would replace the noisy ones. I dreamed of a typewriter that had a screen where the typist could see what was being typed, and the printer would be across the hall in a soundproof room driven by an electrical connection. Before I left the dean's office, an early form of the desktop computer was installed, and a wire was run from the typists' pool to a noisy printer on the other side of the building. Today the desktop computer is much faster, the screen is in color, and the laser printer is silent. I learned that one's dreams can be fulfilled by the genius of others. And the end is not in sight. Computer and other forms of technology will continue to improve.

About twenty years ago a new dream entered my consciousness. It is ongoing and is concerned with less-invasive medical treatments. At the time, my father in his seventies underwent open-heart surgery. I learned that the operation consisted of a large incision from his throat to his midsection followed by the cutting of his sternum with a saw that allowed doctors to open his chest, connect his blood supply to a machine, stop the heart, and perform bypass surgery. Following the operation I stood in the intensive care unit and touched my father's body as they wheeled him to a recovery room. The body was cool and, in some ways, reminded me of a corpse. I had a sense of the trauma that had taken place. From that day onward I have dreamed of less-invasive methods to solve medical problems.

In the intervening years I have watched with interest the progress made by the medical community. Angioplasty is a relatively new procedure for correcting diseased arteries—a method that did not exist twenty years ago. Small balloons attached to catheters can be advanced through an artery over a wire from a small incision in the groin and placed within the arterial and venous system to remove blockages. A small metal tube called a stent can also be placed within the arteries to keep them open. In many cases major surgery is prevented. Another development involves thrombolytic therapy or the ability to dissolve clots. New medicines placed in arteries and veins via catheters are able to dissolve clots, restore blood flow, and prevent amputation. This new therapy also aids stroke patients. Another procedure developed within the last few years is called embolization. A catheter is placed within an artery and chemicals are injected to stop blood flow to tumors or to vessels that are bleeding from trauma. Often tumors that are not surgically removable can be treated in this manner, prolonging the patient's life.[7]

My dream is for the day when doctors will be able to perform medical procedures inside the body using ultrasound or lasers that are relatively noninvasive. Have you ever been to a doctor and wished that she or he could wave a device over you, determine what was wrong, and administer the remedy without invading the skin? Noninvasive medicine is wonderful.

Professor William Pitt of Brigham Young University is developing ways of releasing chemotherapy drugs to specific locations in the body through ultrasound. Chemotherapy can be a miserable experience because, at present, the drug must be administered to the entire body. In Dr. Pitt's work, the drug is bound in inert packages that do not release the drug until ultrasound is administered, and then the drug is confined to a local area. The illness associated with the treatment is thereby reduced.

Another area of current research includes the work in micro-electro-mechanical systems. This interdisciplinary field produces miniature mechanisms the size of a human hair that can travel inside the human body to clean plaque from veins, monitor one's health, or perform microsurgery through remote control. Small microswitches can also be designed for the field of optics, where they are used to drive the small mirrors in a projector to refine the picture and increase the number of pixels used for each color. Another product might be a microsensor used to measure movements of buildings during an earthquake.

Perhaps one's dream might be fulfilled in BYU's Earth Remote Sensing Center, where professors are developing technology and information systems to gather data regarding the earth. Using various forms of radar and other scanning techniques, professors and students are able to locate icebergs, determine wind speeds in storms, produce more accurate weather models, and penetrate the earth's crust to find ancient cities.

Every discipline at this university represents a possible vision or dream. What is yours? Please be aware that it is normal for people's hopes and dreams to shift over time. The choices and opportunities available today may change as time passes. How do you prepare for the opportunities ahead?

To acquire temporal truths, one must be diligent in pursuing an education. To receive spiritual truths, one must be obedient as well as diligent (see D&C 130:19). Spiritual light is received when one follows the doctrine of Christ—that is, the first principles and ordinances of the restored gospel. I challenge you to increase your faith by living gospel principles more precisely, by repenting when you fall short, by taking an active role in your ward, by rendering service to others, and by making prayer and scripture study a part of your everyday life. In this manner you will find true joy.

In closing I turn to the words of the Prophet Joseph Smith, who wrote about the connection between heaven and our intellect as follows:

> We consider that God has created man with a mind capable of instruction, and a faculty which may be enlarged in proportion to the heed and diligence given to the light communicated from heaven to the intellect; and that the nearer man approaches perfection, the clearer are his views, and the greater his enjoyments.[8]

May each of us take advantage of opportunities to educate both our mind and our spirit.

NOTES

1. Merrill J. Bateman, "Learning in the Light of Truth" (paper presented at the Annual University Conference, Brigham Young University, 21 August 2000).

2. *World Book Encyclopedia,* 1974 ed., "The Nature of Light," s.v. "Light."

3. The spiritual spectrum of light is based on statements by Parley P. Pratt in *Key to the Science of Theology,* 9th ed. (Salt Lake City: Deseret Book,

1965), 46–47; and Charles W. Penrose, in *Journal of Discourses,* 26 vols. (Liverpool: F. D. Richards, 1855–86), 26:21–22, 16 November 1884.

4. Charles W. Penrose, in *Journal of Discourses,* 26:21, 16 November 1884.

5. Joseph Fielding Smith, comp., *Teachings of the Prophet Joseph Smith* (Salt Lake City: Deseret Book, 1972), 151.

6. Patricia Farr to Merrill J. Bateman, 7 August 2000, copy of letter in my possession.

7. This information is based on a discussion with Dr. John Collins, an interventional radiologist at Utah Valley Regional Medical Center, 16 September 2000.

8. Smith, *Teachings of the Prophet Joseph Smith,* 51.

CHAPTER 11

"How Knoweth This Man Letters"

(8 JANUARY 2002)

SISTER BATEMAN and I wish to focus on the Savior and the process by which He grew spiritually during His mortal sojourn. The process He followed is no different than the one He has asked us to follow. We hope the presentation will inspire and motivate you to apply the principles outlined.

In the rural towns of Galilee, Jesus often frequented the synagogues and took occasion to teach. He also was well-known as a teacher at the temple in Jerusalem. Each time He taught, those who listened were astonished by His knowledge of the scriptures, the clarity of His doctrine, and the authority with which He spoke. The impact of His teaching is typified by the words of Mark. Mark recorded that during the early part of the Savior's ministry, Jesus went "straightway on the sabbath day . . . into the synagogue, and taught. And they were astonished at his doctrine: for he taught them as one that had authority, and not as the scribes" (Mark 1:21–22).

Jesus' first opportunity to teach in the temple at Jerusalem occurred when He was still a boy. At twelve years of age, He accompanied His parents to Jerusalem where they would participate in the Feast of the Passover to celebrate Israel's deliverance from Egypt. When the time came to return home, Joseph and Mary believed that Jesus was with relatives in another part of the company. After a day's journey they learned that He was not with their kinsfolk, and they returned somewhat agitated to Jerusalem to find Him. After three days of searching, they located Him in the temple, "sitting in the midst of the doctors, and they were hearing him, and asking him questions. And all who heard him were astonished at his understanding, and answers" (JST, Luke 2:46–47).

Even at twelve years of age, His spiritual understanding and maturity were well beyond His years. Eighteen years later, again at Passover, Jesus entered the temple at Jerusalem. On this occasion He cleansed the temple of those selling merchandise and taught the gathered Jews about His impending Atonement, death, and Resurrection by citing scripture (see John 2:13–22). Even those closest to Him, however, did not understand the full import of His sermon until after the Resurrection. But again, they were amazed with His knowledge of the doctrine. On another occasion Jesus returned to Jerusalem to celebrate the Feast of the Tabernacles. Again He taught at the temple. John recorded that the "Jews marvelled, saying, How knoweth this man letters, having never learned?" (John 7:15).

What was meant by this paradoxical question? On the one hand, Jesus demonstrated the same knowledge as a man of letters; but on the other, He had never been formally trained. What did the Jews mean when they said, "How knoweth this man letters?" Those who interacted with Jesus quickly grasped that He was fully conversant with the law, the scriptures, and the doctrine. His knowledge of the prophets and their words exceeded that of the Pharisees and scribes as He confounded them on numerous occasions. On the other hand, the Jews saw Him as one "having never learned." What did they mean by this phrase? Jesus, unlike Paul, had not sat at the feet of Gamaliel or any other celebrated teacher. He had not been a student in the Jewish system of higher education. Therefore, how could He have acquired such profound knowledge?

Sister Bateman and I will address the question of how Jesus grew spiritually and illustrate the importance of searching and pondering the scriptures as part of not only Jesus' spiritual growth but our own. First, Sister Bateman will discuss three ways by which Jesus grew spiritually. Second, I will illustrate the importance of searching and pondering the scriptures as part of the growth process—a process that each one of us must also attempt. Actually there is a fourth element that contributed to Jesus' spiritual maturation that will not be discussed. It is the Atonement— His experience in the garden and on the cross. The Apostle Paul said that Jesus "learned . . . obedience by the things which he suffered" (Hebrews 5:8).[1] In other words, the atoning process was an incredible learning experience.

The Savior's Growth (Sister Bateman)

My subject today concerns the steps taken by the Savior that increased His spiritual understanding and faith. Just as the Lord's physical growth followed a natural sequence, so did His spiritual progress, although the latter was accelerated. What were the key elements that defined the Savior's growth? As John the Baptist stated, "He received not of the fulness at first, but continued from grace to grace" (D&C 93:13). In a similar vein, Luke stated that as Jesus increased in wisdom and stature, He also "increased . . . in favour with God and man" (Luke 2:52). What was the process?

First, like every child, He was taught by His parents. Joseph and Mary had been specially prepared to teach Him. He was in their home and under their tutelage for more than half of His life. They had special knowledge concerning His identity and earthly ministry (see Matthew 1:19–21; Luke 1:29–38). Both of them knew of His divine Sonship. They had been taught by the angel Gabriel of His mission and destiny. They had been taught about His atonement and that He was the Messiah about whom there had been prophecies for centuries. And Mary knew that His mercy and salvation would last "from generation to generation" (Luke 1:50). There can be little doubt Mary and Joseph were knowledgeable and highly effective teachers during the Savior's early years.

Second, knowing the identity of his Father and His purpose on earth, it is reasonable to assume that Jesus learned much through prayer and the power of the Holy Ghost. Undoubtedly He was taught to pray as a young boy—a practice He continued in adulthood. The importance of prayer in His life is illustrated by the fact that His ministry began with forty days of prayer and fasting in the wilderness and concluded with a night of agony and prayer in the Garden of Gethsemane. Often He sought the solitude of the mountains to pray. After one of those private moments, a disciple, having watched Him, pleaded, "Lord, teach us to pray" (Luke 11:1). Jesus clearly pointed out to his listeners that the doctrine He taught was not His but came from God. Only through prayer and the Holy Ghost could He have known this truth. Jesus received the Holy Ghost following baptism and heard His Father's voice declare His divine Sonship. Luke recorded that "the heaven was opened" at this time, which suggests that the Father and the Son enjoyed an intimate relationship (see Luke 3:21).

The Apostle John speaks of this relationship as follows: "God giveth not the Spirit by measure unto him. The Father loveth the Son, and hath given all things into his hand" (John 3:34–35). In other words, Jesus was given "a fulness of the Holy Ghost" following His baptism, indicating that access to the Father was uninhibited (D&C 109:15). The Savior's learning process was orderly in that He received "line upon line, precept upon precept," but the process was accelerated and highly compressed because of His righteousness, talents, and capacities. In contrast, our learning is also "line upon line, precept upon precept," but we are given "here a little and there a little" (2 Nephi 28:30). We are not given all things at once. In contrast to the Savior's experience, the Holy Ghost is given "by measure" to us, and our access to spiritual truth increases as we increase in faith, repent of our sins, and learn to be obedient. For us a lifetime or more may be required to receive the Holy Ghost in its fulness. But again, like the Savior, we do have access to the Holy Ghost to help us grow spiritually.

Third, Jesus was a student of the scriptures. I believe that scriptural study was a major source of His knowledge of spiritual truths. If He was to understand our learning process in mortality so that He could succor us, then it was essential that He learn in like manner. The evidence is strong that He was diligent in searching the scriptures prior to His ministry. Jesus' first sermon in Nazareth is a demonstration of His familiarity with the Old Testament—the scriptures of His day. He deliberately chose Isaiah 61:1–2 to announce His divine Sonship to those in the synagogue. The passage reads: "The Spirit of the Lord is upon me, because he hath anointed me to preach the gospel to the poor; he hath sent me to heal the brokenhearted, to preach deliverance to the captives, and recovering of sight to the blind, to set at liberty them that are bruised, To preach the acceptable year of the Lord" (Luke 4:18–19).

Following the reading, Jesus declared to the congregation that He was the fulfillment of the passage. The Jewish leaders understood the meaning of the verses. They knew that Isaiah's words were a direct reference to the Messiah. For them, Jesus' claim to be the fulfillment was blasphemous. "Is not this Joseph's son?" they declared (Luke 4:22). Jesus then likened Himself to Elijah and Elisha, saying, "No prophet is accepted in his own country" (Luke 4:24–27). Not knowing His true identity, and presuming Him to be an ordinary man, the Jews were enraged by what appeared to them to be blasphemy.

Another illustration of His familiarity with the scriptures is the story of Jesus and the two men on the road to Emmaus following His crucifixion and resurrection. It was Sunday, the day of the Lord's resurrection, and the two men were discussing the recent events in Jerusalem. The Savior approached and joined them. Luke indicated that the eyes of the two men "were holden that they should not know him" (Luke 24:16). Jesus asked them why they were so sad. They in turn questioned Him, suggesting that He must be a stranger in those parts if He was not aware of the events concerning Jesus of Nazareth. The two men then repeated for the Master the particulars of the trial, the Crucifixion, and their disappointment in that they had thought Jesus was the one who would redeem Israel. They concluded by telling the story of His reported resurrection. Women of their company had visited the tomb early that morning and found it empty. Angels reportedly told them that Jesus was alive. They were astonished by the women's report and did not know what to make of it.

After listening to their recitation, Jesus said: "O fools, and slow of heart to believe all that the prophets have spoken: Ought not Christ to have suffered these things, and to enter into his glory? And beginning at Moses and all the prophets, he expounded unto them *in all the scriptures* the things concerning himself" (Luke 24:25–27; emphasis added).

Jesus used the scriptures to teach the two disciples the purpose of His mission and the necessity of His death and resurrection as part of the plan of salvation. The prophetic words of all the Lord's servants had pointed to these three days. All of the prophets from Moses to Malachi had looked forward to the atoning events and had written about them. Later that evening, after the scales had fallen from their eyes and they recognized their Master and Lord, Jesus vanished from their sight. The two men then said: "Did not our heart burn within us, while he talked with us by the way, and *while he opened to us the scriptures?*" (Luke 24:32; emphasis added).

Jesus knew the scriptures. His familiarity with them was earned through study and prayer. He became a student as a boy, and familiarity with the scriptures increased throughout His life. He was the Jehovah of the Old Testament. The heavens were opened to Him because of His righteousness, and His understanding of and familiarity with the scriptures came quickly through prayer and the Holy Ghost.

I testify that scriptural study was a key element in the Savior's growth from "grace to grace" (D&C 93:13), that likewise, time invested in the scriptures will pay huge dividends for us. Our spiritual progress will be shaped by our familiarity with God's words as revealed through the prophets. May each of us commit a few minutes daily to that study.

The Importance of Searching and Pondering the Scriptures (Elder Bateman)

I am grateful to Sister Bateman for her insights. I am inspired by her love for the Savior, and I likewise testify that Jesus was not only a student of the scriptures Himself but has commanded us that we join with Him in that pursuit. He said, "Search the scriptures; for in them ye think ye have eternal life: and they are they which testify of me" (John 5:39).

From the beginning of time God has directed the affairs of His children in mortality through prophets. Their inspiration has been written down for the benefit of the believer. According to the Apostle Paul, these written words have been passed from one generation to another for the purpose of declaring "doctrine, for reproof, for correction, for instruction in righteousness" (2 Timothy 3:16), or, as Christ said, for a testimony of His divinity and understanding of His mission that we might "have eternal life" (John 5:39). By illustration and commentary I wish to help you to appreciate the spiritual power and understanding that await you if you are willing to pay the price of becoming a diligent student of the scriptures.

In a direct statement to the Prophet Joseph Smith, the Lord declared why reading and studying the scriptures can be a revelatory experience. In section 18 of the Doctrine and Covenants, the Lord, speaking of the Book of Mormon and all scripture, said: "These words are not of men nor of man, but of me; wherefore, you shall testify they are of me. . . . For it is my voice which speaketh them unto you; for they are given by my Spirit . . . and by my power you can read them one to another. . . . Wherefore, you can testify that you have heard my voice, and know my words" (D&C 18:34–36).

In this passage the Lord states that when reading the scriptures one may hear His voice, feel His Spirit, and know His words.

Now I turn to the New Testament and the Gospel of John, where we will examine a few scriptures and ponder their meaning in order to understand better the Apostle's message concerning Christ. All of us are familiar with the four Gospels in the New Testament: Matthew, Mark, Luke, and John. The first three are known as the synoptic Gospels because they "see alike"—i.e., they are similar in approach and use much of the same material. These three Gospels bear witness of Christ through a narrative beginning with His birth and ending with His death and resurrection. The Gospel of John, on the other hand, is different. Ninety-two percent of the material in John is not found in the other three Gospels. Rather than telling the story of Jesus' life, John employs key events to teach gospel truths.

The LDS Bible Dictionary indicates that each of the four books was written for a different audience:

> It appears from the internal evidence of each record that Matthew was written to persuade the Jews that Jesus is the promised Messiah. To do so, he cites several [Old Testament] prophecies and speaks repeatedly of Jesus as the Son of David, thus emphasizing his royal lineage. Mark appeals to a gentile audience and is fast moving, emphasizing the doings more than the sayings of the Lord. . . . Luke offers his readers a polished literary account of the ministry of Jesus, presenting Jesus as the universal Savior of both Jews and gentiles. . . . John's account does not contain much of the fundamental information that the other records contain, and it is evident that he was writing to members of the Church who

already had basic information about the Lord. His primary purpose was to emphasize the divine nature of Jesus as the Only Begotten Son of God in the flesh.[2]

As noted, John appears to have been written for members of the Church who have an understanding of basic gospel principles and of who Jesus is. With this context in mind, what did John want the members of the Church to know? We do not have space to discuss the entire book, but a brief review of the first five chapters may be helpful in answering the questions.

The first chapter of John presents testimonies of Jesus' identity. Through the Doctrine and Covenants and the Gospel of John we know that the primary testimonies are those of John the Beloved and John the Baptist (see D&C 93:1–18). A knowledge of the Godhead and the plan of salvation is required to appreciate fully the messages given in this chapter. The first verse of the gospel of John indicates that Jesus was in the beginning, that He was with God, that He was God. To appreciate the meaning of this verse, a knowledge of the premortal world and the relationship between the Father and the Son is necessary. Jesus was the Firstborn in the spirit and lived in the world of spirits with the Father before coming to earth. Because of His righteousness, the light within Him, and His anointing, He was already exalted. As such, Jesus was the Creator of all things, as noted in the third verse. We know through other scriptures, including modern revelation, that Jesus did create all things under the direction of the Father (see Hebrews 1:2; Moses 1:32–33).

Verses 4 through 9 of John 1 declare that Jesus is the source of life and light for every man and woman. We know that the Light of Christ is given to every person who comes into the world to help them know right from wrong. We also know through modern revelation that the Light of Christ is the ultimate source of light and energy for the sun, for the stars, and for this earth (see D&C 88:7–10). Jesus is the source of light and life.

Perhaps the most important verse in chapter 1 is verse 14. It reads: "And the Word was made flesh, and dwelt among us, (and we beheld his glory, the glory as of the only begotten of the Father,) full of grace and truth."

Only Latter-day Saints fully understand and appreciate the meaning of the phrase "the Only Begotten of the Father [in the flesh]." Jesus as a person in the premortal world was the first-born spirit offspring of Heavenly Parents. We also are spiritually begotten by heavenly parents. The difference between our parentage and that of Jesus Christ is that for His mortal advent, Jesus had an immortal Father and a mortal mother. Through Mary, He received mortal seeds that allowed him to die. Through His Father He inherited immortal genes that allowed Him to live forever if He so chose. On one occasion Jesus told the Jews, "For as the Father hath life in himself; so hath he given to the Son to have life in himself" (John 5:26). On another occasion Jesus said: "Therefore doth my Father love me, because I lay down my life, that I might take it again. No man taketh it from me, but I lay it down of myself. I have power to lay it down, and I have power to take it again. This commandment have I received of my Father" (John 10:17–18).

Although the Romans nailed Jesus to the cross, His death was of His own volition. As Paul said, He had "the power of an endless life" (Hebrews 7:16). He did not have to die. He was the Son of an immortal being. His death was a voluntary sacrifice. From His mother He had the power to lay down His life. From His Father He had the power to take it up again. That is why the Atonement is "infinite and eternal" (Alma 34:10, 14). It was performed by an infinite and eternal being. Although there is much we do not understand about the Atonement, a knowledge of Christ's relationship to the Father clarifies the source of his power to accomplish it. Also, a knowledge of the mortality within him helps us appreciate the tremendous pain and suffering He endured to atone for our sins (see D&C 19:16–19).

The first chapter of John concludes with other testimonies that Jesus is the Messiah. John the Baptist identified Jesus as the Lamb of God. In other words, He is the sacrificial lamb for all mankind. Andrew and Philip also bore witness. This wonderful first chapter of John is an introduction to Jesus as the Redeemer of the World. It testifies to us of His divinity and the source of His power.

The second chapter is concerned with Jesus' mission and purpose on earth. He is the promised Messiah whose mission is "to bring to pass the immortality and eternal life of man"—to accomplish the Atonement (Moses 1:39). Two key statements in the second chapter illustrate that Jesus knew at the beginning of His ministry what the end would be. The story used by John to illustrate these truths is the marriage feast at Cana.

Jesus and His disciples entered Cana on the third day of the week to attend a marriage celebration to which they had been invited. During the feast the host and hostess ran out of wine. The Savior's mother then approached Jesus and asked for help. His response was: "Woman, what wilt thou have me to do for thee? that will I do; for *mine hour* is not yet come" (JST, John 2:4; emphasis added).

Jesus agreed to the request made by His mother but noted that His actions would relate to His hour, even though that hour had not yet come. What was Jesus' hour? In numerous references it is the time in the Garden of Gethsemane and on the cross. His hour is the time during which He performed the Atonement (see John 12:23; 17:1).

After asking the servants to fill six waterpots to the brim—waterpots used for cleansing and purifying—He told them to "draw out" and take to the governor, who then asked why the "good wine" had been kept until now. John then stated, "This beginning of miracles did Jesus in Cana of Galilee, and *manifested forth his glory;* and his disciples believed on him" (John 2:11; emphasis added).

As stated earlier, the glory of the Father and the Son is to bring to pass the immortality and eternal life of man. How did the conversion of water to wine relate to His hour? What did the conversion signify? What did the wine represent?

There are a number of parallels that might be drawn. The power to convert water to wine might parallel the power of Christ's atonement to change men and women from mortal to immortal beings, to transform corruptible bodies into incorruptible ones, to create an inseparable connection between body and spirit in the Resurrection (see 1 Corinthians 15:42–44; D&C 93:33–34). In short, the miracle at Cana not only illustrated Christ's power to change the earthly element of water to wine but also His power to "cleanse" and "purify," to lift men and women from mortality to immortality—from an earthly to a celestial state. In this way, the miracle was connected with His hour and did show forth His glory.

The third chapter of John is concerned with the introductory ordinances of the gospel. After introducing Christ in chapter 1 and confirming the purpose of His mission in chapter 2, John turned to the basic ordinances required for members to participate in the blessings of the Atonement. The story is that of the Jewish leader Nicodemus coming to Christ by night, asking what he must do in order to enter into the kingdom of God. He is told that he must be born again of water and of the Spirit. That is, he must be baptized by immersion for the remission of sins and receive the gift of the Holy Ghost.

Chapter 4 then describes what a member following baptism must do to stay on the path to eternal life. This chapter tells the story of Christ meeting the Samaritan woman at the well and telling her of living water that quenches one's thirst forever. Christ is the Fountain of Living Waters, and those who drink from the well of His goodness, mercy, and teachings will never thirst. The water is a symbol for His gospel, the "good news . . . that Jesus has made a perfect atonement for mankind that will redeem all mankind from the grave and reward each individual according to his/her works" (Bible Dictionary, "Gospels"). The water is also linked to the sacrament in our day, which reminds us that we must internalize His words and the Atonement by taking His name upon us and by keeping His commandments.

The fifth chapter of John is the story of Jesus healing the sick at Bethesda. For me the story has great meaning. The scriptures read:

> Now there is at Jerusalem by the sheep market a pool, which is called in the Hebrew tongue Bethesda, having five porches.
>
> In these lay a great multitude of impotent folk, of blind, halt, withered, waiting for the moving of the water.
>
> For an angel went down at a certain season into the pool, and troubled the water: whosoever then first after the troubling of the water stepped in was made whole of whatsoever disease he had.

And a certain man was there, which had an infirmity thirty and eight years.

When Jesus saw him lie, and knew that he had been now a long time in that case, he saith unto him, Wilt thou be made whole?

The impotent man answered him, Sir, I have no man, when the water is troubled, to put me into the pool: but while I am coming, another steppeth down before me.

Jesus saith unto him, Rise, take up thy bed, and walk.

And immediately the man was made whole, and took up his bed, and walked. (John 5:2–9)

Why did John include this story in his gospel? To what ordinance, covenant, or promise does this miracle refer? Will there come a day when Jesus tells each of us to rise, walk, and be made whole? One of the great blessings that awaits all mankind is the glorious Resurrection, the opportunity to be redeemed from the bands of physical death—a time when each person will be given power to restore the "sleeping dust . . . unto its perfect frame, bone to his bone, and the sinews and the flesh upon them" (D&C 138:17). As Jesus lifted the blanket of despair from the lame man, so He will lift in a future day from each of us the blanket of the grave, allowing us to rise in a newness of life through the power of His atonement and resurrection. When that day comes, no man or woman will be able to say, "I have no man to help me!" As the lame man at Bethesda was made whole, so we in the Resurrection will experience the greatest healing of all as "spirit and element, inseparably connected, receive a fulness of joy" (D&C 93:33).

The 1883 Carl Heinrich Bloch painting of *Christ Healing the Sick at Bethesda* now hangs in the BYU Museum of Art. It is a masterpiece, depicting the Lord as healer and comforter both in time and eternity. I encourage you to ponder its message. (See frontispiece of this book.)

Do you feel the beauty and power of the scriptures? Can you sense the blessings that await if you drink deeply of Christ's living water? Will you set aside a few minutes each day to read from the scriptures and then ponder the meaning of the verses read? When the day comes for us to stand before the keeper of the gate, the Holy One of Israel, it is my prayer that He will not perceive in us a slowness of heart to believe that which the prophets have said. Rather, may He see us as men and women of spiritual letters, having learned day by day over a lifetime. May each of us so prepare to meet Him.

NOTES

1. The JST indicates that this verse applies to Melchizedek and not to Christ. However, Melchizedek is a type for Christ (see Alma 13), and the principle stated is applicable to the Savior as well (see Alma 7:11–12).

2. LDS Bible Dictionary, 683, s.v. "Gospels."

CHAPTER 12

Temples of Learning

(10 SEPTEMBER 2002)

T OMORROW IS THE one-year anniversary of the terrible events
that occurred in New York, Washington, D. C., and Pennsylvania,
when terrorists hijacked four airplanes in an attempt to rob
America of its safety and security. On 11 September 2001, Sister
Bateman and I were scheduled to give the first devotional of the
school year. We awoke early to prepare for the day. During the
morning we turned on the television to listen to the news. It was
not long before the cameras shifted to New York City and the
north tower of the World Trade Center, which had just been hit.
The announcer noted that an airplane had crashed into the tower,
puncturing the building just below the 100th floor. They were
uncertain as to whether it was an accident or a deliberate act. A
short time later, while the cameras were still focused on the twin
towers, another plane came into view headed for the second tower.
What followed was an unbelievable sight. United Flight 175 continued its course, crashing into the south tower. At that point it
was apparent that the acts were deliberate, the planes had been

hijacked, hundreds of lives had been taken, and thousands were in danger. The floors that had been hit became drenched with airplane fuel, and soon the towers were raging infernos in the upper reaches of the buildings. All of us watching feared for the lives of those who were on the upper floors. Little did we understand what was about to happen. Within an hour the blazing heat generated by the fireball melted the steel infrastructure, bringing the south tower crashing to the ground. The north tower followed twenty-nine minutes later.

As Sister Bateman and I watched, we became concerned about the students at BYU. It did not seem appropriate to move forward with the regular devotional, but we felt a strong need to gather the BYU community together to briefly discuss the events and then counsel together regarding the challenges that lay ahead. In the special devotional one year ago, we indicated that there was no reason to fear for our lives or the lives of loved ones unless they were in the planes or at the sites of impact.[1]

We also noted the importance of being respectful of all people. On campus we have students from most countries. How important it was then and now to be kind and considerate of every individual. For thousands of years innocent people have been ill-treated because of ethnicity, nationality, or religious persuasion. Our own history reveals the ignorance and intolerance endured by our ancestors as they were driven from Missouri to Nauvoo and then the Rocky Mountains. Intolerance on this campus is an anachronism—something entirely out of place, something not suited to this location. This campus is and must continue to be a haven of peace and understanding where each individual is seen and treated as a child of God.

On the occasion of that terrible act of terrorism, we stated that the only answer to these horrible events is the "good news"—the gospel of Jesus Christ. This earth will find peace only when its citizens come to know the Prince of Peace. But we need not wait for others to find peace. By living the gospel each of us may receive an inner assurance that all is well. We have access to the Holy Ghost, who is the Comforter. Near the end of the Last Supper, Jesus turned to His disciples and said, "Peace I leave with you, my peace I give unto you: not as the world giveth, give I unto you. Let not your heart be troubled, neither let it be afraid" (John 14:27). Even though He knew of the agony and trial of the next few hours, Jesus told His disciples that they would find peace. As Latter-day Saints, we are part of the greatest mission for peace the world has ever known.

Looking back, what are the lessons learned? The first is that we can make the world safer than it was, but it is not easy to root out evil when a small group of people separate themselves from civilized society, are well funded, live in a wilderness, and strike with an element of surprise against innocent people. The Book of Mormon tells about a similar terrorist group and the chaos that ensued when the general society also turned away from God. Fortunately, we know that in the last days the kingdom of God will not be destroyed but will spread across the earth—touching every nation, kindred, tongue, and people and preparing the earth for the return of its Creator. In the long run, al-Qaeda will not succeed.

A second lesson was taught by the New York firefighters and policemen who put duty before life. As the occupants of the towers were coming down the stairwells, they met the firemen going up. A new set of heroes was born. Recently an eight-year-old boy was leaving Shea Stadium in New York after a Mets baseball game. As he was crossing the street, he saw a police officer directing traffic. The boy approached him and asked the officer if he would sign his baseball glove.

The policeman looked at the young boy and said, "Don't you want a ballplayer's autograph? Why a cop's?"

The boy answered, "Because you saved the world."

There is a greater respect and awareness today for those civil servants who risk their lives in the course of duty.

Another lesson comes from the testimony of Church members who lost loved ones. Sister Mary Alice Wahlstrom and her daughter were on American Flight 11 from Boston to Los Angeles when it was diverted by hijackers and flown into the north tower of the World Trade Center. Almost a year later Margaret Wahlstrom, Sister Wahlstrom's daughter-in-law, stated the following: "I wish I could give everybody a testimony of the gospel. You're taught all these things throughout your life, and all of a sudden you have to live them. When something bad happens, you find out how strong your testimony is and if you believe in the Atonement—and you find out that you do."[2]

There are some problems associated with the events of 9/11 yet to be resolved. The World Trade Center has been cleaned up, but some people still live in fear that another tragedy will occur. Al-Qaeda's forces have been reduced, but pockets of terrorists remain and continue to plan events. The world economy, although headed into recession prior to 9/11, was dealt a severe blow by those events and is still trying to recover.

On the other hand, the civilized world is more unified than before, more willing to stand together against those who would destroy our way of life. And from the ashes of last September has arisen a stronger America—one more committed to freedom, one more caring of those in need. Perhaps most important of all, a younger generation has been exposed to acts of war and tyrants who want to force their beliefs on others. The events of 9/11 will always be a warning in their memories that freedom is not guaranteed but must be protected. Finally, many people have been led to ask questions about the purpose of life and are searching for answers.

Temples of Learning

Now I turn to my main topic: temples. I wish to share with you my view of BYU as a temple of learning. I also wish to point out that you, as individuals, are holy temples of God yourselves and therefore should protect your bodies and souls because they are sacred. The dictionary defines a temple as "a building or place dedicated to worship or the presence of deity." As you know, LDS temples are dedicated homes to deity. On every temple appear the words *House of the Lord.* LDS temples are also places where sacred priesthood ordinances are performed. Temples in our religion have three major purposes.

The first is to provide men and women with a vision of their eternal potential.

The second is to provide instruction as to how we can achieve the goals God has set for us.

The third is to link us through ordinances and covenants to the grace and power of Christ's Atonement so that we may receive a fulness.

Now, consider how BYU might be a temple of learning. Is it a home for deity? Does it have a responsibility to help young people understand their potential in both mortality and eternity? Does it have a sacred as well as a secular responsibility to help you reach your ultimate destiny? Is there power in teaching you how to learn and providing you with knowledge concerning heaven and earth?

The answer to each question is, "Yes!" Brigham Young told Karl G. Maeser that Brigham Young University was to be a home for the Holy Spirit.[3] This member of the Godhead should be present in every classroom and pervade the university. His presence softens and enhances relationships between faculty and students and affects student-to-student relationships as well. His presence also enhances the learning process. The seeking of knowledge—both temporal and spiritual—is a sacred responsibility given to every woman and man. On this subject the Lord has said:

"And I give unto you a commandment that you shall teach one another the doctrine of the kingdom.

"Teach ye diligently and my grace shall attend you, that you may be instructed more perfectly in theory, in principle, in doctrine, in the law of the gospel, in all things that pertain unto the kingdom of God" (D&C 88:77–78).

The scripture then shifts to secular matters:

"Of things both in heaven and in the earth, and under the earth; things which have been, things which are, things which must shortly come to pass; things which are at home, things which are abroad; the wars and the perplexities of the nations, and the judgments which are on the land; and a knowledge also of countries and of kingdoms" (D&C 88:79).

And then the Lord indicates why we are to learn both spiritual and secular subjects: "That ye may be prepared in all things when I shall send you again to magnify the calling whereunto I have called you, and the mission with which I have commissioned you" (D&C 88:80).

Everyone reading this message has been called by the Lord to a special mission. The more we know about things in heaven and in the earth, the more effective we will be in accomplishing the commission given us. The aims of a BYU education are designed to this end. They are to increase your intellectual capacities and understandings, to enlarge you spiritually, to build your character, and to help you become lifelong learners and lifetime servants.

During a freshman orientation, I shared one of the most sacred moments I have experienced on this campus because it illustrates the blessing and power of this university as a temple of learning. Prior to the dedication of the Palmyra New York Temple, First Presidency instructions were for students to gather in local Provo chapels to view the services. After some investigation it was determined that few students would be able to attend because local Saints would fill the chapels. Consequently I asked President Hinckley if the services could be shown in the Marriott Center. Although there was some concern that it would be difficult to feel the spirit of the services in such a large space, permission was granted.

Students with recommends were asked to be in their seats at least thirty minutes before the services began. The outside doors of the building were locked twenty minutes before. I arrived early and took a seat on the floor. As I entered through one of the tunnels, I immediately noticed the extreme quiet in the room. There were no sounds. There was no whispering. Almost every student had a set of scriptures, and each was quietly reading or pondering the events of the next two hours. A quiet, reverent attitude prevailed throughout the dedication. Following the dedicatory prayer, 20,000 students stood in this arena and with white handkerchiefs waving repeated the Hosanna Shout. It was electric! The sea of handkerchiefs was like fields of grain waving in the wind. I have attended a number of temple dedications, but not one like that.

Following the closing hymn and prayer, the Holy Spirit pervaded every corner of the arena. We watched on the screen as President Hinckley and others departed the celestial room of the

Palmyra Temple. I then approached the microphone and excused those in attendance to return to their classes. The few of us on the floor stood and waited for the audience to leave. But no one moved. After another minute or two I returned to the microphone again and invited those in attendance to return to class. Slowly, quietly, people arose and left the building. It was one of the great, spiritual moments of my time at the university. The building, used on other occasions for events totally unlike what we had witnessed, literally became an extension of the Palmyra Temple during those two hours.

I now understand better the dream given to Karl G. Maeser in the 1880s when he said: "I have had a dream—I have seen Temple Hill [upper campus] filled with buildings—great temples of learning, and I have decided to remain and do my part in contributing to the fulfillment of that dream."[4]

Brigham Young University is a great temple of learning. Each building has been dedicated to the Lord as a house of learning. The university will fulfill its destiny.

I noted earlier that each of us is a temple of God. Our bodies have been so designated because they are designed to house the Holy Ghost as well as our own spirits. In scripture, Jesus was the first to speak of the body as a temple. After cleansing the Jerusalem temple of the money changers and merchants, the Jews asked Jesus for a sign of His authority. He said to them, "Destroy this temple, and in three days I will raise it up" (John 2:19). His Jewish inquisitors thought He was referring to the building, but we know that He was referring to His body.

Writing to the Corinthians, the Apostle Paul described sexual sin as a sin against one's own body and then used the temple metaphor to indicate the seriousness of such acts. He said: "What? know ye not that your body is the temple of the Holy Ghost which is in you, which ye have of God, and ye are not your own? For ye are bought with a price: therefore glorify God in your body, and in your spirit, which are God's" (1 Corinthians 6:19–20).

To some the last sentence may seem strange. If we own anything on this earth, one would expect it to be our body and our spirit. In a sense that is true. We are our own person. But Paul is pointing out that Christ's atonement determines what we become. We still have our agency, but He paid for our future possibilities. In that sense *He* owns us. We still must submit to Him. We still must give ourselves to Him.

In the garden and on the cross, the Savior's atonement made possible our sanctification through the power of His blood and the help of the Holy Ghost. If we strive to live the gospel, our bodies become temples in which the Spirit of God resides. The price paid by the Savior ensures that our bodies and spirits will overcome death and be raised to a higher state. By living close to the Holy Ghost, the day will come when we will be changed from mortals to immortals, and our souls will receive a celestial glory. In terms of everything that counts, Christ owns us.

For these and other reasons, we must treat our bodies with the utmost care. The world does not understand what we have just discussed. It does not understand the Atonement. It does not appreciate the sacred nature of the body. Not only does the body house the Holy Spirit, but it also contains the sacred power of life. The power to give life is a godly power granted to us for a season. How we protect and use it is of utmost importance to our salvation.

When we understand that the body is a temple, we will not deface it. When we understand the sacredness of the body, we will understand the importance of modest dress. We will understand the incongruity of individuals stripping to the waist and painting their faces and bodies at football games. We will do all in our power to stay away from pornographic materials of all kinds. In this regard, one of the most serious challenges facing young people today, especially young men, is pornography. It is more addictive than cocaine. Do not take it into your temple. It has the power to destroy you. It destroys relationships between men and women. It distorts values and pollutes the mind. Stay away from it. If you know of anyone caught in this mire, do not pass them by. Insist that they get help. People caught in this web find it very difficult to break the chains that bind them, but there are professionals who can help.

May I thank you for the exceptional people you are. An integral part of the life of this university is the presence of the Holy Ghost abiding in you. Brigham Young University is a temple of learning. We are temples. The Lord told Joseph Smith that every person is entitled to a gift of the Spirit (see D&C 46:11). As we assemble in the weekly devotional, each person brings a gift that can be shared with others. That is how we become a Zion people. That's why we have wards and stakes, so we can share those gifts. No wonder the alumni tell us that the most important activity on campus for their spiritual development was the weekly devotional. I promise all who come a clearer vision of their destiny and more power to achieve it.

In conclusion, may we remember and honor those whose lives were lost in last year's tragedy. May we live in a manner that will add to the Spirit in this temple of learning. May each of us be worthy receptacles of the Holy Ghost.

NOTES

1. Merrill J. Bateman, "Hope for Peace," *BYU 2001–2002 Speeches* (Provo, Utah: Brigham Young University, 2002), 95–96.

2. "Legacy of Good, Absence of Hate," *Church News,* September 7, 2002, 3.

3. See Alma P. Burton, *Karl G. Maeser: Mormon Educator* (Salt Lake City: Deseret Book, 1953), 26.

4. From Ernest L. Wilkinson and Leonard J. Arrington, eds., *Brigham Young University: The First One Hundred Years,* 3 vols. (Provo, Utah: Brigham Young University Press, 1976), 3:3.

The Gospel of
Jesus Christ

CHAPTER 13

One by One

(9 SEPTEMBER 1997)

I WOULD LIKE to share an experience that illustrates a principle the Lord uses to direct His work. The story concerns a young woman who desired to attend BYU from the time she was very young but believed she would never have the opportunity because of difficult financial circumstances. Consequently she did not apply during her senior year in high school even though her grades were excellent and she was worthy.

As is customary, university advisement personnel hold meetings for newly selected freshmen each spring. On the day this meeting was held in her hometown, the young woman received in the mail a notice that she was a National Merit finalist. This meant her tuition would be paid by a national scholarship. Still, she did not have the financial means to cover the additional costs associated with moving from home and living in another state and city. However, the confluence of the notice and the meeting for new BYU freshmen rekindled a spark of hope, and she decided to attend even though she was not on the invitation list.

I happened to be in the city that day on other business and was invited by our advisement people to speak to the new freshmen at the evening gathering. Following the main session, the freshmen were divided into small discussion groups and sent to other parts of the building. As I left the chapel, I stopped momentarily to visit with waiting parents. While conversing, I suddenly felt the presence of someone behind me. The feeling was followed by an impression that my help was needed. I turned, and there stood two women a few feet distant quietly conversing. They noticed my movement and looked up. I could tell they were waiting to see me. As I approached them, the mother introduced herself and indicated that her daughter would like to ask some questions. The young woman told me of her lifelong dream to attend Brigham Young University and how because of financial circumstances she had not applied. She then proceeded to tell me of the letter that had arrived that day notifying her of the National Merit Scholarship. She further stated that even though her tuition would be paid, her circumstances were such that it still appeared impossible to attend. She then asked if I knew of any way a door might be opened. As I listened, the thought came that her hope had been rekindled by the Holy Spirit and that I had been made aware of her presence by the same source. Additional thoughts came regarding university resources, including student jobs that are available. With the help of BYU admissions personnel, a way was found for the young woman to attend.

I recently received a short note from her. It has prompted me to speak on the subject I have chosen. The note read as follows:

Dear President Bateman,

I would like to thank you for sharing my story [at freshman orientation]. I came here feeling lost and lonely and a little bit without purpose. I cannot tell you how I felt when I realized you were talking about me. I know God wants me here, and I know I am here to serve Him. Thank you![1]

The note bore the signature of the young woman.

As I reflected on her letter, I realized that all of us feel lonely, lost, and weighed down at times. It is not a freshman phenomenon. It is part of life. It is part of the "opposition in all things" (2 Nephi 2:11). For that reason, I want my young friend and all of you to know that we are not alone. First, Brigham Young University is a family. It is a community of close friendships, of brothers and sisters who share testimonies and values and who treasure each other. In this regard I was impressed with an article in a recent edition of the *Daily Universe,* written by a professor on campus. The article was about a student friend whose life was taken in a tragic automobile accident. In concluding the article, Professor Rudy stated:

> I hope students can learn from Lindsay to dare to have conversations with their professors. We want to talk with you about our courses but also about the problems and challenges in your lives, about the big and important decisions you are making, about your hopes and dreams. . . . Together, here and now, we can continue to help each other attain the experiences and learning that will help us fulfill our missions in this life and in the life to come.[2]

Given the special nature of the university, there are many friends who will listen, provide counsel, and share your hopes and dreams. In addition to faculty, staff, and fellow students, bishops wear a special mantle and are entitled to the gift of discernment in your behalf.

Second, there is a special friend who knows us intimately, who stands by us in critical moments, and whose request is that we come to know Him and His Father (see John 17:3). He is the Lord Jesus Christ. His sojourn in mortality and His atoning experience provide Him with unique insights regarding our challenges, sorrows, and infirmities. As Paul testified, we worship a Savior who has a "feeling of our infirmities" (Hebrews 4:15), who has "compassion" for us because He was "compassed with infirmity" (Hebrews 5:2). His personal knowledge, His great love, and His atoning powers combine in tailoring His assistance to meet our peculiar needs. To honor the gift of agency, He invites each person to come to Him and establish a "one by one" relationship through the Holy Spirit (see John 16:12–14; 3 Nephi 11:15; 17:21). There are two passages in the Book of Mormon that clearly illustrate the level of His personal interest and many passages that provide understanding regarding His awareness of our problems and willingness to help. Let me share a few passages with you.

During the Savior's visit to the Nephites in the Western Hemisphere, He told them that He had "drunk out of that bitter cup" (3 Nephi 11:11). He then extended the following invitation to the multitude gathered: "Arise and come forth unto me, that ye may thrust your hands into my side, and . . . feel the prints of the nails in my hands and . . . feet, that ye may know that I am the God of Israel, and the God of the whole earth, and have been slain for the sins of the world" (3 Nephi 11:14).

The record indicates that the multitude went forth "*one by one* until they had all gone forth, and did see with their eyes and did feel with their hands, and did know of a surety" (3 Nephi 11:15;

emphasis added). Although the multitude totaled 2,500 souls, the record states that "all of them did see and hear, every man for himself" (3 Nephi 17:25). If each person were given fifteen seconds to approach the resurrected Lord, thrust their hand into His side, and feel the prints of the nails, more than ten hours would be required to complete the process.

The record indicates that later the Savior "took their little children, *one by one,* and blessed them, and prayed unto the Father for them" (3 Nephi 17:21; emphasis added). The scriptures do not indicate how many children were there, but one surmises that in a multitude of 2,500, there must have been a few hundred. Again, it would have taken hours to give each one a blessing.

Why did Jesus take the time to invite each individual to feel the wounds in His hands and feet and put their hand into His side? Why did He bless each child rather than give a collective pronouncement? Would the personal touch of His hands and the power of His Spirit be more efficacious in a "one by one" relationship? The answer is given by the Savior Himself when He said: "And ye see that I have commanded that none of you should go away, but rather have commanded that ye should come unto me, that ye might feel and see; even so shall ye do unto the world" (3 Nephi 18:25).

Suppose you had been in Bountiful that day and experienced a "one by one" relationship with the Savior of the world. You would have fallen at His feet. You, too, would know that He had drunk out of the bitter cup. You would feel some responsibility for the prints of the nails in His hands and feet and the wound in His side. You would have seen the engraving of your image in "the palms of [His] hands" (1 Nephi 21:16). On occasion, speakers note that the impact of His appearance produced a season of peace that lasted two hundred years. The truth is that His appearance and teachings had an *eternal* impact on the lives of those present and for generations to come.

The Savior's "one by one" invitation is consistent with the principle that salvation is an individual matter. The saving ordinances are administered "one by one." Baptism, confirmation, and priesthood ordinations are performed individually. Missionaries are sent "two by two" to teach individuals and families and baptize "one by one." Home teachers and visiting teachers are sent to "visit the house of each member" (D&C 20:47). Although the highest exalting ordinances are administered "two by two" and in families, saving covenants administered one person at a time form the foundation. The gospel plan provides for each individual to receive his or her own witness (see Alma 32; Moroni 10:3–5). Men and women are expected to know for themselves. More than that, the Savior knows each of us for who we are. As Paul told the Corinthians, "Now I know in part; but then shall I know even as also I am known" (1 Corinthians 13:12).

There were many years in which I believed that the atoning process involved an infinite mass of sin being heaped upon the Savior. As I have become more familiar with the scriptures, my view of the Atonement has changed. I now know the Atonement involved more than an infinite mass of sin; it entailed an infinite stream of individuals with their specific needs. Alma records that Jesus took upon Himself the pains, afflictions, temptations, and sicknesses of His people. In addition, He experienced their weaknesses so that He would know how to help them (see Alma 7:11–12). Isaiah prophesied that the Lord would bear "our griefs, and [carry] our sorrows"; that He would be "wounded for our transgressions" and "bruised for our iniquities" (Isaiah 53:45). Paul explained to the Hebrews that Jesus tasted "death for every man" and woman (Hebrews 2:9). No wonder "his sweat was as it were great drops of blood" coming from "every pore" (Luke 22:44; D&C 19:18). Isaiah and Abinadi stated that when "his soul has been made an offering for sin he shall see his seed" (Isaiah 53:10; Mosiah 15:10). And who are His seed? Those who follow the prophets (see Mosiah 15:11–17).

Know this: the Atonement was not only infinite in its expanse but intimate in the lives of God's children. The Redeemer of the world is acquainted with each person's infirmities. He knows your problems. He understands your joys as well as your sorrows. He knows the nature of the temptations that beset you and how they interface with your weaknesses. Above all He knows you and knows how and when to help you. Generally His help is given through the Holy Ghost. The Holy Spirit speaks quietly by generating thoughts and feelings within. The promptings received for the young woman wanting to study at BYU were not happenstance. I do not know what the Lord has in store for her, but I do know that her desires to attend this university were understood by Him.

Do you understand the process by which you "come to Christ" in order to know Him and His Father? I suspect you do! Nevertheless, I wish to review four important steps every person must follow in order to nurture a "one by one" relationship with the Savior.

The first step is to believe in Him and to exercise faith in His character and being by praying to the Father in His name.

The second involves becoming familiar with His words, His promises, and His covenants.

The third is to ponder His teachings and internalize and live them.

The fourth is to follow the Savior by serving the one, by

showing respect to each and every person, and by obeying the commandments.

During the Savior's visit to the Nephites, He instructed them that they were to pray always so they would not enter into temptation. He warned them that "Satan [desires] to have you, that he may sift you as wheat" (3 Nephi 18:18). The word *sift* means to separate or divide. There is strength in unity. Beware of the world's philosophies that claim to be unifying but are divisive. If Satan can separate an individual from the righteous influence of his or her family and the Church, the person becomes vulnerable to temptation. Satan's most effective tool is to teach a person not to pray (see 2 Nephi 32:8). Alma promised his son Helaman that if he would counsel with the Lord in all his doings both morning and night, he would be lifted up at the last day (see Alma 37:37). Prayer is a master key that opens heaven's door. It also opens the door to one's own heart and gives the Holy Spirit access.

Faith in Christ grows as we become familiar with the Lord's teachings and apply them in our lives. Alma teaches that if a person plants the word of the Lord in his or her heart and then nurtures the seed, it will grow into the tree of life with all the fruits thereof (see Alma 32). The Savior told Joseph Smith that those who study the scriptures will hear His voice, feel His Spirit, and know His words (see D&C 18:34–36). Just as study of academic subjects expands one's mind and provides tools for earthly success, so a study of eternal truths expands one's soul and provides the strength to be successful in heavenly things.

When Nephi wanted to understand his father's dream, the scriptures state that he pondered the meaning in his heart (see 1 Nephi 11:1). Deep spiritual understanding does not come through casual thinking or study. Profound mental searching is required. Often, spiritual insights come after we have done all that we can do and then with the aid of the Spirit. It is important that we take a few minutes each day to review our lives, reflect on our spiritual status, make the necessary adjustments in order to stay on the "strait path" (2 Nephi 33:9), and recommit to be obedient to the commandments.

Finally, we must serve one another by showing respect for each person and by helping those in need who cross our paths. Nephi states that the Lord invites "all to come unto him and partake of his goodness; and he [denies] none that come . . . black and white, bond and free, male and female" (2 Nephi 26:33).

There is much we can learn from one another, "for there is no respect of persons with God" (Romans 2:11). The Master does not hold one of us above the rest. He loves each man and woman and asks us to do the same. The prophet Alma asked the following question: "Is there one among you that doth make a mock of his brother [or sister], or that heapeth upon him persecutions? Wo unto such an one, for he is not prepared, and the time is at hand that he must repent or he cannot be saved!" (Alma 5:30–31)

We ask men and women to honor each other. Each woman and man "has the right and the responsibility to direct her [or his] own life."³ Each person is of infinite worth as measured by the plan of mercy. Christ suffered for and experienced the pains of "every living creature, . . . men, women, and children" (2 Nephi 9:21).

Several years ago Marilyn and I attended a district conference in Kanazawa, Japan. The theme for the Saturday evening session was "The Atonement of Christ." We spoke about the Savior's sacrifice, His knowledge concerning each person, His invitation to have a "one by one" relationship, and His desire to help each individual overcome the trials and temptations in his or her life. At the end of the Sunday session, a young Japanese woman sought me out. She wanted to share a special experience she had had during the morning session. While listening to the sermons, she had reflected on the message of the previous evening. Suddenly she realized that the Savior knew her. He knew how she felt about the gospel. He could read the thoughts and feelings that were hers. With tears rolling down her cheeks, she told how wonderful it was to know that the Savior of the world knew her.

May each of us accept the Savior's invitation to approach Him and to spiritually see and feel the wounds in His hands, feet, and side. May we exercise faith in Him as the Redeemer of the world. May we honor Him by loving one another as He loves us.

NOTES

1. Personal correspondence in my possession.

2. Jill Terry Rudy, "Student's Death Teaches Lessons of Life," *Daily Universe* (Provo, Utah), 4 September 1997, 4.

3. Spencer W. Kimball, *My Beloved Sisters* (Salt Lake City: Deseret Book, 1979), 23.

CHAPTER 14

The Eternal Family

(6 JANUARY 1998)

In a Saturday evening session of a stake conference in New York, I listened intently to a young Hispanic sister bear her testimony. As a recent convert she bore witness of the promptings and feelings that occurred during her conversion. She stated:

> When the missionaries knocked on my door, I saw the smiles on their faces and felt the firm grip of their handshakes. They said they had a message that would bring happiness into my life. At the conclusion of the first lesson they turned to Moroni's promise in the Book of Mormon. I was surprised. They did not ask me to believe their words. Instead, the missionaries challenged me to find out for myself the truthfulness of the gospel through prayer and the Holy Ghost. Later, as I listened to the missionaries explain the plan of salvation, I suddenly felt a confirming witness that I was more than a speck in the universe. My life was important not only to me but to a loving Heavenly Father and his Son. They knew me!

There was purpose to life, and God had a plan for me to achieve that purpose. I could never feel worthless again![1]

The truth of the young sister's testimony burned within me that evening. I knew then, and know now, that there is purpose to life, that God has a plan of happiness designed for all of His children. The plan includes a premortal existence in which men and women were begotten spirits, "born of heavenly parents, and reared to maturity in the eternal mansions of the Father, prior to coming upon the earth in a temporal body to undergo an experience in mortality."[2] Individuals were blessed with the gift of agency in premortal life just as they are here. Those spirits who were obedient to law gained knowledge and intelligence and were rewarded with a second estate. One's progress depended on the choices made (see Abraham 3:22–26; Moses 4:14; Revelation 12:39). Agency always has been an integral part of the plan (see D&C 93:30–31, 38).

Mortality and the Formation of Eternal Families

The plan includes an earthly or temporal sojourn as well. During this state we receive a physical body with procreative powers and the opportunity to form eternal families of our own. The power to create new life is given to men and women for a season, and they are tested as to how they will use this sacred power. By the time death occurs, the power is removed. For those obedient to eternal law, the procreative power is restored in the Resurrection. For those who are disobedient to righteous principles and are unrepentant, the power is never returned (see D&C 131:14; 132:22, 25).

A key purpose of God's plan is the formation of eternal

families. It is within the family that exaltation is achieved. I am aware that some individuals do not have the opportunity to marry in mortality. For those who remain single on earth, there is still much that can be done to develop one's talents, to help others, and to prepare for the blessings that will come. For the promise is that no blessing will be withheld eternally if a person is worthy.[3]

The creation of the earth, the fall of Adam, and the atonement of Christ are essential elements or pillars in the Father's plan for the progress and development of His children. This is true not only for the salvation of the individual but for the exaltation of the family. The earth's creation provided a new state of existence apart from our spiritual home, and mortality's probationary test is qualitatively different from the premortal one. It differs in that we are expected to live by faith. A veil has been drawn over our minds, and we remember little or nothing of life with our Heavenly Parents. In the words of Ecclesiastes, "There is no remembrance of former things" (Ecclesiastes 1:11). In Paul's words, "For now we see through a glass, darkly" (1 Corinthians 13:12). Through faith, assurances come (see JST, Hebrews 11:1). But diligence and obedience are required to hear and feel the still small voice.

The test in mortality also differs because the physical body is subject to a set of desires and temptations. Mortals by nature have an "inherent . . . inclination to succumb to the lusts . . . of the flesh [and] the allurement of worldly things."[4] The earthly test is whether we will yield to the seductions of nature or to the "enticings of the Holy Spirit," which changes our nature "through the atonement of Christ" (Mosiah 3:19). Alma's counsel to Shiblon was to "bridle all your passions, that ye may be filled with love" (Alma 38:12). As children and parents, a family setting allows us to love, trust, care, and serve in a different environment.

The fall of Adam made it possible for children to be born and, therefore, families to be created (see 2 Nephi 2:23, 25). The atonement of Christ opens the door of salvation for the individual and exaltation for the family (see D&C 131:14; 132:22). The three doctrinal pillars of the plan of salvation—the Creation, the Fall, and the Atonement—are intimately involved in the creation of eternal families and their extension into the eternities.

Creation of Man and Woman

The scriptures state that men and women are created in the image of God (see Genesis 1:26–27; Abraham 4:27–28). Both women and men have within them the attributes of divinity, and both are blessed as they fulfill their divine callings. The Apostle Peter and King Benjamin indicate that we partake of the divine nature through Christ's atonement aided by the Holy Ghost (see 2 Peter 1:38; Mosiah 3:19). It is interesting to observe the similarity of the fruits of the Spirit to the divine seeds (love, joy, peace, faith, and so on) inherited from Heavenly Parents (see Galatians 5:21–22; 2 Peter 1:38). Since "light cleaveth unto light" and Spirit to spirit, the Holy Ghost is able to quicken us by a portion of light that causes the divine seeds within to bud and to flower (see D&C 88:29, 40). The degree of light and the extent to which the attributes flourish is a function of how well women and men bridle their passions and are obedient to divine principles.

When a man understands how glorious a woman is, he treats her differently. When a woman understands that a man has the seeds of divinity within him, she honors him not only for who he is but for what he may become. An understanding of the divine nature allows each person to have respect for the other. The eternal view engenders a desire in men and women to learn from and share with each other.

Men and women are created as complements. They complete one another. Paul told the Saints of his day: "Nevertheless neither is the man without the woman, neither the woman without the man, in the Lord" (1 Corinthians 11:11). Men and women complement each other not only physically, but also emotionally and spiritually. The Apostle Paul taught that "the unbelieving husband is sanctified by the wife, and the unbelieving wife is sanctified by the husband" and through them both the children are made holy (1 Corinthians 7:14). Men and women have different strengths and weaknesses, and marriage is a synergistic relationship in which spiritual growth is enhanced because of the differences.

The Family Proclamation

In September 1995 the First Presidency and the Council of the Twelve Apostles issued "The Family: A Proclamation to the World."[5] The document is an extraordinary statement outlining Church doctrine with respect to the family and the relationships between husband and wife, parents and children. On a number of occasions, President Gordon B. Hinckley has been asked why the proclamation was issued. Typical of his answers is the following:

> Much of the world is in serious trouble over the disintegration of the family. The family is the basic unit of society. No nation is stronger than the homes of its people. . . .
> Lawrence Stone, the noted Princeton University family historian, says: "The scale of marital breakdowns

in the West since 1960 has no historical precedent that I know of, and seems unique. . . . There has been nothing like it for the last 2,000 years and probably longer." You are familiar with the fruits of broken homes. I think the home is the answer to most of our basic social problems, and if we take care of things there, other things will take care of themselves.

We are trying to preserve the traditional family—father, mother, and children—working together in love toward a common goal. In large measure we are succeeding against great odds.[6]

Following the issuance of the proclamation, all members of the Church have been challenged to become familiar with its doctrines and teachings and to apply them. It is particularly revealing to compare the teachings of the proclamation with contrasting philosophies and practices of the world. A review of the world's practices regarding marriage and the family illustrate the challenges that beset a society when it loses its eternal compass. May I share with you the basic principles taught by the proclamation and contrast them with the beliefs and practices that are becoming more and more prevalent in society. In doing so, I am aware that there are many people outside the Church who value the traditional family and whose views are similar to ours relative to this important institution. Nevertheless, the data suggests that the family is under siege in America and the Western world.

Marriage between a Man and Woman Is Ordained of God

The first principle taught by the proclamation is that "marriage between a man and a woman is ordained of God." We believe that the first marriage was performed by God and that marriage had no end (see Genesis 2:22–24; Moses 3:21–24). Marriage is a sacred relationship. When performed in the right place by the right authority, an everlasting covenant is established between the man, the woman, and the Lord (see D&C 132:15–19). The covenant has the potential of creating an eternal unit.

We believe that society has a stake in marriage in that the physical, emotional, spiritual, and economic health of its citizens is determined by the quality and duration of marital relationships. We believe that procreative powers are sacred and are to be used only between a man and a woman legally and lawfully married. It has been clearly demonstrated that when these powers are used outside of marriage they destroy relationships rather than build them and have the potential to wreak social havoc, spread disease, and spawn unhappiness.

In contrast, many people in the world treat marriage as merely an association by consenting adults.[7] The association may or may not be based on a contract. Sexual relationships outside the association are widely seen as acceptable. Open marriages without a contract are more and more prevalent as young people live together on a trial basis. Some people are now asking that an association between partners of the same sex be recognized as marriage. It is clear that marriage is not considered a sacred relationship in many quarters. In fact, some argue that the state or society has no interest or stake in marriage.

The Family Is Central to the Father's Plan for the Eternal Destiny of His Children

The second principle taught by the proclamation is that the family is central to the Father's plan for the destiny of His children. As noted earlier, the plan calls for mortal probation and the testing of God's spiritual offspring (see Abraham 3:22–26). In the testing process the family is essential for the proper training of children in the faith (see D&C 68:25, 28). The commandment that God gave to Adam and Eve to "multiply, and replenish the earth" remains in force (Genesis 1:28; Moses 2:28). Father and mother are important role models in nurturing and developing children. We believe that children's self-respect and identity are partially determined by the love their father and mother have for each other. President David O. McKay often repeated the saying, "A father can do no greater thing for his children than to let them feel that he loves their mother."[8] My experience suggests that a child's identity and feelings of security are threatened when parents argue and condemn one another. The home is the best place for children to experience the bonds of love and learn virtue, honesty, and good citizenship. The home is the primary place where children learn to treat others with respect.

What are the world's views with regard to the family? There are many who assume that there is no plan because there is no God. Life is an accident. Marriage and the family are temporal associations. The association between consenting adults has as its purpose pleasure and individual satisfaction. If the association no longer serves that purpose, it should end regardless of the impact on one's partner or children. Is it any wonder that marriages do not last given these views? More than half of all civil marriages in the United States end in divorce. Based on these philosophies, it is not difficult to propagate an argument recently heard in a Hawaiian court that children can be nurtured as well by two adults of the same sex as by the natural father and mother.[9] Also, if marriage is a temporary association that may end at any time, it is then simple to extrapolate that governments should assume primary responsibility for children's training and education.

In a general conference address, Elder Bruce C. Hafen pointed to the Savior's comments on the "contractual attitudes" of the "hireling" versus the covenant relationship of the shepherd: "When the hireling 'seeth the wolf coming,' he 'leaveth the sheep, and fleeth . . . because he . . . careth not for the sheep.' By contrast, the Savior said, 'I am the good shepherd, . . . and I lay down my life for the sheep.'"[10] When the view is myopic, the distortions are large. When one's marital objectives are selfish and transitory, relationships are ephemeral.

One can assume that the longer the view a woman and man have regarding the marital relationship, the greater the probability of success. The divorce rate for temple marriages is well below that of civil marriages, and civil divorce rates are exceeded by separation rates for so-called open marriages.[11] A view of marriage and the family based on eternal principles increases the probability of success. When one takes the long view, one tries harder to be patient, long-suffering, kind, gentle, and meek. These characteristics, in turn, strengthen the marriage.

Principles and Practices That Build Successful Families

The proclamation teaches that "successful marriages and families are established and maintained on principles of faith, prayer, repentance, forgiveness, respect, love, compassion, work, and wholesome recreational activities." In other words, the Lord measures the success of a family by the quality of its relationships. In a home where faith, love, and forgiveness are dominant, members find joy and satisfaction in being together. Ideally the father presides in love and righteousness, provides the necessities of life, and protects the family while the mother is primarily responsible for the nurturing of the children. In contrast, the world often measures family success by the accumulation of worldly things and the size of the estate that is passed on to the children.

Many programs and practices in the Church are designed to strengthen the family. These include family home evening, family councils, family history work, family prayer, father's blessings, family scripture study, and others. It is important for families to build special traditions that tie children to parents and grandchildren to grandparents. In closing may I share one of the family practices that has produced joy and pleasant memories in our family. It is a tradition that has tied us together as a nuclear and an extended family.

When our oldest children were ready to begin formal schooling, Sister Bateman and I decided that a father's blessing would be given to each child and to the mother at the beginning of the school year. The family home evening preceding the start of school would be the occasion. We began the practice when Michael, our oldest son, turned five and was about to enter kindergarten. The practice continues to this day, although there is only one son at home. He is a student at BYU. When all the children were home, eight blessings were given on that special Monday evening.

The year Michael was about to enter the third grade holds poignant memories for us. During the summer he had participated in Little League baseball. He was a backup catcher and an outfielder on his team. For his age he had some athletic ability and was a good player. At the time he loved baseball. When we gathered together for family home evening just before the start of school, Michael announced to the family that he was too old for a father's blessing. After all, he had completed his first season in Little League, he had played well, and blessings were for younger children.

Marilyn and I were stunned at first. We encouraged him by suggesting that a blessing would help him with his schoolwork. It would provide him with protection. It would help him in his relationships with his brothers, sisters, parents, and friends. But our encouragement, along with considerable coaxing and cajoling, failed. He was too old. Since Marilyn and I believe in agency and were not about to force a blessing on an eight-year-old, all of the children except Michael received a blessing that year.

The school year proceeded normally. Michael and the other children did well and the family enjoyed their associations together. As the following May arrived, it was time for Little League baseball to begin. Following the last day of school, Michael's coach called a team practice. Michael's anticipation could not have been greater. His dream was about to be realized. He was to be the starting catcher. The baseball diamond was located in the river bottoms not far from the mouth of Provo Canyon and a few blocks from our home. The boys and the coach walked to the field. Following the practice the boys and coach started for home. Michael and a friend decided to run on ahead of the coach and the other boys. In the process they had to cross University Avenue not far from the mouth of the canyon. As they approached the highway, Michael's friend looked each way and noticed a car coming from the north. Michael failed to look and darted onto the highway just as a sixteen-year-old boy, out for his first drive in his brother's car, came speeding out of the canyon.

I can't imagine the fear that must have struck the young driver's heart as he saw the small boy in front of him. The driver slammed on the brakes and swerved in an attempt to miss the boy.

The side of the front fender and grill hit Michael and threw him down the highway, where he landed in a heap of broken bones.

Sister Bateman and I were visiting parents in American Fork when the police reached us by telephone with the news. We were told that Michael was in an ambulance on his way to the hospital and that he was in critical condition. Before leaving American Fork, I called a friend and asked him to meet us at the hospital to assist in giving Michael a blessing. The drive from American Fork to Provo was the longest twenty minutes of our lives. During the drive Marilyn and I prayed fervently, asking the Lord to preserve the life of our son and bless me with an understanding of the Lord's will for him. In those twenty minutes we learned what it means to pray with "real intent" (Moroni 10:4).

As we parked the car by the door of the emergency room, we saw the police and a young man leaving the hospital. He was crying. The police recognized us and introduced us to the young man as the driver of the car. We put our arms around him and told him that we knew it was not his fault. We then entered the hospital to find Michael. We found him in a room with doctors and nurses feverishly attending to his needs. He had received a concussion and was irrational and crying for his mother. His scalp was laid back on his head, and the broken bones were obvious. My friend had arrived, and we asked if we could have two or three minutes with him alone before they took him to the operating room. They agreed. Again I prayed with all the fervency of my being that his life would be preserved and that the blessing would reflect the Lord's will. My friend anointed and I sealed. As I laid my hands upon his head, a feeling of comfort and peace came over me. Words flowed and promises were made.

For the next four weeks Michael lay in a hospital bed with his head bandaged, his arm in a cast, and his leg in traction. Each

Wednesday evening following the Little League game, his teammates would file into the hospital room and give Michael a rundown. Each week tears would well up in Michael's eyes and run down his cheeks as he saw his teammates enter the room and heard the boys relive the game. He would have given anything to be able to participate. After four weeks Michael was put in a body cast that went from his chest to his toes. On two or three occasions we took him to a game to watch his friends play. Another four weeks passed, and the body cast was replaced with a cast from his hip to his toes. Two days before school was to begin, the cast was removed, and Michael began the long process of exercising his leg to obtain full use again.

As the family gathered the next night for school blessings, is there any wonder as to who wanted the first blessing? A nine-year-old boy, a little older and a lot wiser, was first in line. Michael is not the only member of our family to learn from the experience. All of the other children have talked about the protection offered by a father's blessing. Over the years they have come to understand that accidents are not always prevented by priesthood blessings, but they have also learned that more than one type of protection is available through the priesthood. Today our grandchildren are recipients of priesthood blessings. The tradition is in its second generation. We hope that this practice, like the family, will prevail through the eternities.

It is my testimony that the family is meant to be eternal. Each one of us may be part of an eternal family if we are obedient to gospel principles. A fullness of joy is found only within the framework of an exalted family. Some people may scoff at the seventh commandment, which requires chastity before marriage and fidelity afterward, but the world's ways are not a substitute for the plan of happiness. Marriage is a sacred relationship between a man and a woman. May each of us live so that we may partake of the greatest blessing the Lord has in store for us, that of eternal life.

NOTES

1. Notes in author's possession. The young woman's name is Luce Gonzales, and the conference was held in Rochester, New York.

2. "The Origin of Man," November 1909, in James R. Clark, comp., *Messages of the First Presidency of The Church of Jesus Christ of Latter-day Saints,* 6 vols. (Salt Lake City: Bookcraft, 1965–75), 4:205.

3. See Clyde J. Williams, ed., *The Teachings of Harold B. Lee* (Salt Lake City: Bookcraft, 1996), 256.

4. Bruce R. McConkie, *Mormon Doctrine,* 2nd ed., rev. (Salt Lake City: Bookcraft, 1966), 781, s.v. "temptation"; see also Alma 42:10.

5. "The Family: A Proclamation to the World," *Ensign* 25 (November 1995): 102.

6. Gordon B. Hinckley, *Teachings of Gordon B. Hinckley* (Salt Lake City: Deseret Book, 1997), 209–10.

7. See Bruce C. Hafen, "Covenant Marriage," *Ensign* 26 (November 1996): 26–28.

8. See *Teachings of Gordon B. Hinckley,* 201.

9. See Brief for Amici Curiae Bronfenbrenner et al., Baehr v. Miike, No. 91–1394–05 (Haw., 23 May 1997).

10. Hafen, "Covenant Marriage," 26; see also John 10:12–15.

11. See Tim B. Heaton and Kristen L. Goodman, "Religion and Family Formation," *Review of Religious Research* 26, no. 4 (June 1985): 343–59; John O. G. Billy, Nancy S. Landale, and Steven D. McLaughlin, "The Effect of Marital Status at First Birth on Marital Dissolution Among Adolescent Mothers," *Demography* 23, no. 3 (August 1986): 329–49; Larry L. Bumpass and James A. Sweet, "National Estimates of Cohabitation," *Demography* 26, no. 4 (November 1989): 615–25.

CHAPTER 15

Lay Hold upon Every
Good Thing

(18 SEPTEMBER 2001)

On September 11, 2001, tragedy struck our nation. The events of that day have had an impact not only on the United States but on the entire world. Most governments now realize that no one is safe if terrorists are allowed free rein to develop secret networks and plan strikes against innocent people. It reminds one of the Gadianton robbers, who lived in a day long ago. The Book of Mormon indicates that they were experts in wickedness, lived in the wilderness, operated through secret combinations in the settled parts of the land, and were difficult to find and destroy (see Helaman 2:4, 11; 3:23). Could there be a more apt description of the enemy we are now facing?

These terrorist acts have sobered everyone and caused us to reflect on the sanctity of life. The tragedy has made clear that, for many, the most important aspect of life is found in family relationships. In the midst of the rubble, rescuers have uncovered the dead clutching family photos. One man who escaped from the collapsing towers indicated how grateful he was that he could hug his children one more time. The last words heard from a husband to his wife were "I love you!" And then there are men and women, young and old, waiting near the crash sites displaying pictures of their loved ones and hoping for a miracle. Someone has said that God will turn the evil into good. If the citizens of this and other nations recognize their frailties and turn to God for help, good will be the outcome.

However, experience indicates that transformations are seldom permanent unless one is deeply touched by the Holy Spirit. Clearly, given our understanding of the plan of salvation, the importance of family, and the eternal destiny of man, Latter-day Saints will have a much different perspective on these events than those who do not share our faith. Speaking to BYU students on the day of the attack, I told them that they (the young people) held the power of peace for the world in their hands and that the world depended on them. (See chapter 9 of this book.) The fact is, Christ depends on not just the students, but all of us who are members of His Church. The message of the Master must be written in our hearts so that we may extend it to others. Christ's healing power is more than physical. He has the power to make a person whole, to heal the spirit as well as the body.

Sister Bateman and I approach this topic with concern, knowing and feeling the responsibility that is ours to teach and uplift. The theme we have chosen is taken from the seventh chapter of Moroni, wherein Mormon explains that "the Spirit of Christ is given to every [person], that [they] may know good from evil" (Moroni 7:16). Mormon then counsels the Nephites to "search diligently in the light of Christ . . . and . . . lay hold upon every good thing" (Moroni 7:19).

Given the events of 9/11, we wish to discuss the opportunity members of the Church have been given to search in the light and to lay hold upon good things that bring lasting happiness. Young adults, particularly, are in the midst of the most critical decision-making period of life. If you are a young person, it is especially important that you have the light and faith to make right decisions, to discern good from evil, to hold onto and develop the things that the Lord has in store for you. It is interesting that Satan offered Adam and Eve the opportunity to know good and evil (see Genesis 3:5). In contrast, Mormon indicates the purpose of mortality is to help us to "know good *from* evil" (Moroni 7:19; emphasis added). One can know evil without tasting it.

I ask you to consider a Minerva Teichert painting called *Lehi's Dream* (see frontispiece of this book), which illustrates in a particularly graphic way the importance of making right choices. The painting is of Lehi's dream of the tree of life. I would like to draw your attention to the large and spacious building with its gold dome, statues, and multitudes of people. One would think that it is the most important symbol in Lehi's dream. Even though it is in the background of the painting, it is so bright and inviting that it commands attention and attempts to overshadow other parts of the story. The building rises up from the water, having no foundation, and a careful examination reveals that blue sky pierces the open door and windows. As Professor John Welch and Doris Dant note, "The great building is merely a facade with the sky showing through the door and windows, appropriate for a symbol of the pride and 'vain imaginations' of the world (1 Nephi 12:18)."[1] The real story is in the foreground. It is the pathos of a family struggling to hold onto good things, to find their way to the tree of life and to partake of its fruit. Two sons have left the safety of the path and iron rod, whereas others continue the journey. I believe the tree is a symbol for Christ, and the fruits of the tree are the blessings of the Atonement. You will note in the painting that the tree is not highlighted. It is off to the side and in the shadow of the building. Sister Teichert knew that in life it is easier to follow the crowd and the ways of the world than it is to discipline one's appetites along the strait and narrow road to life. As Jesus said: "Enter ye in at the strait gate: for wide is the gate, and broad is the way, that leadeth to destruction, and many there be which go in thereat: Because strait is the gate, and narrow is the way, which leadeth unto life, and few there be that find it" (Matthew 7:13–14).

With the painting as a figurative metaphor, what are the good things we must grasp and internalize? I would like to recommend three things worth seizing: The first is to make a commitment to build an eternal family and thereby establish your eternal identity. The second is to maintain your personal purity. The third is to learn by study and by faith. Sister Bateman will discuss the first objective.

The Importance of Eternal Families (Sister Bateman)

For the last forty-two years, my major interest and focus have been the creation of an eternal family. I believe it is the most important mission a man or woman can pursue. When one realizes that Heavenly Father's work and glory is to raise and educate children, one can understand why I believe that my work has been in partnership with Him and why it is the most exciting work on earth. If earthly parents are wise and desire a fullness of joy, they will strive to emulate our Heavenly Parents. Many of the lessons needed in this life and in the next are learned in the family setting. That is why I determined many years ago to focus my energies on the greatest calling of all—to be a mother, wife, and daughter in

Zion. I recognize that not all have the opportunity in this life to be a mother or father. But everyone is a son or daughter, and most are a sister or brother, an aunt or uncle. Everyone plays a role in an earthly family, and everyone may build an eternal family.

My subject today centers on the family. Some of you may feel that the decisions regarding a companion and starting a family are a few years away. But you are an important part of your parents' family, and the choices you make today and in the near future will affect personal family decisions later. For others, spousal and parental decisions are already upon you.

Building Eternal Families (Sister Bateman)

Minerva Teichert's painting of Lehi's vision and the tree of life reminds us of the importance of having a vision of what life can be. This includes the vision of a family in the eternities. It is important to set goals, establish priorities, and then "hold fast [to] that which is good" (1 Thessalonians 5:21). The painting illustrates the importance of family relationships and the challenges that can come. The family of Lehi and Sariah, depicted in the painting, is a type for all families. Lehi and his family's journey to the promised land is symbolic of our journey through life. Our ultimate goal is to obtain an inheritance in the heavenly city. In the painting, Lehi is depicted inviting his family to come to the tree and partake of the fruit of eternal life. He is inviting them to come to Christ and build an eternal family. The decision regarding one's spouse is the second-most important decision in life. It is second only to the decision to follow Christ.

Sisters, suppose you have found a wonderful companion, as Sariah had found Lehi, and then one day he arrives home from work and announces that the family should leave for an unknown city. Your nice home and all that is in it will be left behind, and your future living arrangements are uncertain. He asks you to organize the children and bring the scriptures, a few clothes, and some food. What would your answer be? Suppose your husband indicates that an angel has appeared to him and has told him to leave! Would your answer change? Trust between husband and wife is a most valuable possession. Living the gospel together is your only protection. My advice to you is to find a companion who will live the gospel and be worthy of your trust!

Husbands, suppose the day comes when you have a dream and your wife agrees to support you. But the dream takes longer to fulfill than you expected, and there are unforeseen trials along the way. Again, living the gospel and focusing on an eternal family will sustain you in facing and overcoming such challenges.

The painting illustrates the tender feelings that parents have for children and how anxious they are to have all of them complete the journey. Most of us are familiar with the story and are aware of the conflict that exists. Laman and Lemuel resisted the counsel of their parents, but Nephi and Sam learned for themselves that their father spoke the truth (see 1 Nephi 2:16). In spite of the expressions of love and the pleadings to "rebel no more" (2 Nephi 1:24), Laman and Lemuel ended up rejecting the gospel and choosing the ways of the world.

In the Teichert painting, the prophet Lehi has arrived at the tree and is partaking of the fruit. Holding to the rod with one hand, he offers fruit in the other and invites his family to come and partake. Sariah, the mother, is in the foreground, almost overcome with both joy and sadness. First, dropping to her knees in a sign of humility, she recognizes the tree as a symbol for Christ. Second, she sees Laman and Lemuel in a small boat making their way to the large and spacious building. In the process of losing two sons, she pleads with them to return while pointing to the tree. Nephi, knowing his mother's sorrow, holds the rod in one hand and reaches down with the other to help her. How important it is for children to support their parents!

Family relationships are important and crucial to a child's development. Children need parents and parents need children. Brothers and sisters play a vital role in the faithfulness of other siblings. Sister Teichert illustrates the importance of one brother strengthening another by showing Sam holding onto Nephi. In contrast, Laman and Lemuel do not provide leadership for their brothers and sisters. As Lehi learned of Laman and Lemuel's fate through the dream, he "feared lest they should be cast off from the presence of the Lord" (1 Nephi 8:36). Nevertheless he continued to counsel and work with them. As a parent he never gave up on his children. The scripture reads, "And he did exhort them . . . with all the feeling of a tender parent, that they would hearken to his words" (1 Nephi 8:37). Parents never give up.

Family relationships are sacred. The bonds within families have spiritual roots. We know that we lived as brothers and sisters before coming to earth. More important, we are aware that families formed on earth can be eternal. The doctrine that eternal life is familial is central to the gospel of Jesus Christ and therefore one of the unique teachings of our church. Families are welded together by covenant in love and service to each other. As Nephi is reaching out to assist his mother, he is demonstrating sympathy and understanding for her grief. Love is a spiritual gift and comes from the light within us. It is expressed through the service we render. Christ's life is the epitome of service and reflects His love for everyone. Families are built through service: parents to children early in life and then children to parents later. President Spencer W. Kimball said, "God does notice us, and he watches over us. But it is usually through another mortal that he meets our needs. Therefore, it is vital that we serve each other."[2]

And the mortals who serve us are often in the family. A few experiences in my life have taught me the truth of President Kimball's statement. I know that Heavenly Father is aware of families and that He will prompt one family member to meet the needs of another. Some years ago the Lord helped me in a time of trial as He directed our family in the support of my parents. More than twenty years ago, President Bateman and I lived in New Jersey with our children. My parents lived in Provo. My father was in very poor health.

At the time my husband was working for a large, multi-national firm and had just been promoted to a senior position. In the previous three years we had moved from Utah to England and then to Pennsylvania. Now the new assignment was causing us to move again, this time to New Jersey—the third move in three years. The children had patiently accompanied us, adjusting to new schools and establishing new friends each year. We bought a new home in a beautiful area of the state and settled down for what we hoped would be a long stay. We had no desire to move again.

We had been in New Jersey only a few months when BYU president Dallin H. Oaks called and asked my husband to serve as dean of the School of Management. Neither of us felt that another move was appropriate. The children were adjusting to their new environment, Merrill was happy in his work, we had just received callings in the ward and stake, and we were becoming acquainted with our neighbors. Consequently, we declined the offer. During the next few months President Oaks contacted President Bateman on a number of occasions and asked if there was any chance that he might change his mind. After the third or fourth time, the Spirit touched my husband, and he knew that we should accept the BYU position and return to Provo. I agreed to the move, but I was uneasy and concerned for the children. Although I prayed for peace regarding the move, no confirmation came, and I wondered about the change.

One night a few weeks before we were to leave for Provo, I had a dream that awakened me in the middle of the night. In the dream I was terribly upset because my father was dying and I was unable to return home. I awakened my husband and related the dream to him. After some discussion we felt that it was the Lord's way of assuring me that the decision to move was right.

A few weeks later we arrived in Provo, where we were glad to be with our parents again. We enjoyed spending time with them and renewing family relationships. One month after our arrival we were visiting my parents when my father began having chest pains. Mother rushed him to the hospital, but by evening Dad was gone. The experience of losing a parent is traumatic. I will never forget the sadness I felt, but I remembered the dream and now more fully understood its meaning and purpose. The month prior to my father's death was an important time for our children to become reacquainted with their grandfather and for Merrill and me to express our love and support for both Dad and Mom. It was also important that we were there to support my mother in a time of great need. In the months that followed, our appreciation for the Lord deepened as we knew He was aware of us and had prompted us to change our course. As He had done with Lehi and Sariah, He was willing to help in the building of an eternal family.

Family relationships are sacred and are meant to be eternal. Each person in a family is important, as evidenced by last week's disaster. Each person is needed to complete the family circle. The absence of a person may leave a huge crater in the hearts of family members.

Hold tightly to the iron rod. Pray that you might discern good from evil. Build strong family ties. Keep in contact with your parents and grandparents, "search diligently in the light of Christ" and "lay hold upon every good thing."

Gratitude for Families (President Bateman)

I am grateful for Sister Bateman's role in our family. She has a sixth sense when it comes to building relationships. We now have twenty-five grandchildren. Someone asked my wife a short time ago if she knew all of their names. She was stunned and surprised by the question. Not only does she know their names, birthdays, and upcoming events concerning them, she has a personal relationship with each one. After all, they are her children, too. Whenever grandchildren visit our home, they head for the library to find Grandma, who is often reading. It is wonderful to see them embrace her and for Sister Bateman to gather the little ones in her arms. She plans family events that bring grandparents, children, and grandchildren together to build relationships. Remember, when you form your own family, find ways to bind your children and grandchildren to you. And at this stage of your life, spend time with parents and grandparents before it is too late. The greatest good on this earth and in eternity is the family.

You are at a critical juncture in life. Your temporal dependence on parents is diminishing, but do not let the spiritual links weaken. As President Gordon B. Hinckley noted in a recent BYU devotional, you must "never become a weak link in the chain of your family's generations."[3]

Personal Purity

Now I come to the second challenge. The creation of an eternal family depends on personal purity. This earth was created for three major purposes. The first was to allow us, God's spirit children, to obtain a physical body. The second was to test our obedience to eternal laws. The third was to create an eternal family. The three purposes are linked. You cannot accomplish the third, that is, an eternal family—without achieving the first two. On occasion while teaching a religion class, I have asked students why it is necessary to have a body. Generally the answer is "to become like God." I then ask, "Why does God have a body?" Often there is silence, suggesting they do not know.

The physical body is essential to the creation of life. As spirit children we could not form families of our own. We did not have the power. The seeds of life are in the physical tabernacle. Perhaps that is an additional reason why our bodies are called the temple of God. Paul stated that the physical body is a temple of God because it is a house for the Holy Ghost (see 1 Corinthians 6:19–20). The sacred power of creation is given to us for a relatively short time—for only a few decades—and then removed. We are given laws and tested to see if we will respect this power, protect its use, and respect the body. If we are obedient, the power of life returns in the Resurrection. If we abuse the power and do not repent, the natural capacity to create never returns, and we live singly in the eternities (see D&C 131:14–17).

In a classic devotional given at BYU a few years ago, Elder Jeffrey R. Holland gave three reasons why sexual intimacy must be saved for marriage. In order to appreciate the reasons, one must understand the sacredness of life. The giving and taking of life are sacred parts of the Lord's plan. Sexual sin is second only to murder (see Alma 39:5). As Elder Holland states:

> Clearly God's greatest concerns regarding mortality are how one gets into this world and how one gets out of it. These two most important issues . . . He . . . wishes most to reserve to Himself. These are the two matters that He has repeatedly told us He wants us never to take illegally, illicitly, unfaithfully, without sanction.[4]

Given the sacredness of life, the first reason that sexual purity is so important relates to the doctrine of the soul. We are taught that "the spirit *and* the body are the soul of man" (D&C 88:15; emphasis added). And, in Elder Holland's words: "When one toys with the God-given . . . body of another, he or she toys with the very soul of that individual, toys with the central purpose and product of life. . . . In trivializing the soul of another . . . we trivialize the atonement, which saved that soul and guaranteed its continued existence."[5]

The second reason is that human intimacy is a sacred "symbol of total union."[6]

The final reason for moral purity given by Elder Holland is that "sexual union is . . . a [union] of the highest order, a union not only of a man and a woman but very much the union of that man and that woman with God."[7]

Do you see the links between personal purity and eternal families? Please understand how important it is not to swim in the river of filthy water seen by Nephi. As sure as the Mississippi River flows into the Gulf of Mexico, so the river of filth flows into the "gulf of misery" (see 1 Nephi 15:27–28; 2 Nephi 1:13). Commit to lay hold upon a life of personal purity that you may have the power to build an eternal family.

Learn by Study and by Faith

Finally, I encourage you to dedicate yourselves to a lifetime of learning in the light—to learn by study and by faith. The most important function of Brigham Young University is to provide you with an enlightened environment. I have heard some complain—primarily people outside the Church—that this campus does not provide enough choice. Since choice is made possible by opposites, the logical conclusion of their statement is that there is too much light at BYU and not enough darkness. They seem to suggest that we should "search in the dark"—at least part of the time—to prepare for the "real" world. Last week's events suggest that there is enough evil in the world without inviting it into our lives. Moreover, Mormon's words suggest that one need not partake of evil in order to gain knowledge.

The truth of the matter is that temptation can find a person anywhere. Satan's work knows few boundaries. He has a long history of playing with the emotions and physical desires of young people. He will tempt you in your relationships, through television, movies, magazines, the Internet, and e-mail. He knows how to invade your apartments and homes. He will not forget you!

So, regardless of where you are, search in the light. It is better to search in the light of day assisted by knowledgeable friends than at night with Lucifer holding the flashlight. From my perspective, this campus is an enormous opportunity for young people to learn from the experience of others, to explore new ideas, to be supported by colleagues who desire only the best. It is a blessing to be surrounded by good people when making eternal decisions.

In the end, the opportunity to acquire spiritual knowledge will depend on your sensitivity to the Spirit. This type of learning cannot be forced. The Lord will determine the time and place. If you are diligent, new truths will enter your mind and heart, you will "feel pure intelligence flowing into you," there will be "sudden strokes of ideas . . . presented unto your minds," and you will have been taught by the Holy Spirit.[8]

In light of the events of 9/11, the words of President Harold B. Lee seem appropriate. In a memorable devotional talk called "Have Faith in America," given on 26 October 1973 at Ricks College, President Lee said:

> Men may fail in this country, earthquakes may come, seas may heave beyond their bounds, there may be great drought, disaster, and hardship, but this nation, founded on principles laid down by men whom God raised up, will never fail. This is the cradle of humanity, where life on this earth began. . . . This is the place of the new Jerusalem. This is the place that the Lord said is favored above all other nations. . . . Yes, . . . men may fail, but this nation won't fail.[9]

May we be true to the Light and to the principles of freedom, justice, and mercy.

NOTES

1. John W. Welch and Doris R. Dant, *The Book of Mormon Paintings of Minerva Teichert* (Provo, Utah: BYU Studies; Salt Lake City: Bookcraft, 1997), 60.

2. Edward W. Kimball, ed., *The Teachings of Spencer W. Kimball* (Salt Lake City: Deseret Book, 1982), 252.

3. Gordon B. Hinckley, "Keep the Chain Unbroken," *BYU 1999–2000 Speeches* (Provo, Utah: Brigham Young University, 2000), 111.

4. Jeffrey R. Holland, *Of Souls, Symbols, and Sacraments* (Salt Lake City: Deseret Book, 2001), 67.

5. Holland, *Of Souls, Symbols, and Sacraments,* 13.

6. Holland, 17.

7. Holland, 17.

8. Joseph Fielding Smith, comp., *Teachings of the Prophet Joseph Smith* (Salt Lake City: Deseret Book, 1972), 151.

9. Harold B. Lee, *Ye Are the Light of the World* (Salt Lake City: Deseret Book, 1974), 350–51; see also L. Brent Goates, *Harold B. Lee: Prophet and Seer* (Salt Lake City: Bookcraft, 1985), 557–59.

CHAPTER 16

Mortality and Our Eternal Journey

(14 JANUARY 2003)

THE SPAN between birth and death is short, whether we live to be twenty or one hundred. On the other hand, in spite of its brevity, life's purposes and consequences are profound in the span of eternity. Sister Bateman and I wish to discuss the mortal journey, its purposes and challenges, and its role in the eternal plan.

Sometimes when I ponder and review my life, I wonder what it would have been like to have lived in the time of the Savior and to have been in His presence. Would I have recognized the special nature of His being (see Matthew 22:42)? Would I have had sufficient faith to be healed by a touch of His garment (see Matthew 14:35–36)? Or if I had been in the synagogue in Capernaum and heard His declaration of His true identity, would I like the others have murmured at the strictness of the way "and walked no more with him" (see John 6:51–66)? If the Pharisees and Sadducees had threatened me, would I have denied knowing Him out of fear for my own safety? These questions and their answers generally leave me a little unsettled.

I have recently given some thought to another question and its answer: a question Pilate asked Jesus and the answer given by the Savior. After the chief priests and leaders of Jerusalem had taken counsel to put Jesus to death, they took Him to Pontius Pilate with the hope that the governor would approve and implement the sentence, since the Jews did not have the authority to execute capital punishment (see John 18:28–31). During the interview, Pilate asked Jesus:

"Art thou the King of the Jews? . . .

"Jesus answered, My kingdom is not of this world: if my kingdom were of this world, then would my servants fight, that I should not be delivered to the Jews: . . .

"[Not fully understanding the response, Pilate restated the question:] Art thou a king then? Jesus answered, Thou sayest that I am a king. To this end was I born, and for this cause came I into the world, that I should bear witness unto the truth" (John 18:33, 36–37).

As I have pondered Pilate's question and the Savior's answer, I have come to realize their importance. They are classic. "Who am I? To what end was I born? For what purpose came I into the world?"

Sister Bateman and I will explore these questions: Who are we? Why are we here? What are the purposes of this mortal sphere and what are the challenges of the mortal journey? We hope we will add to your knowledge and provide incentive for each to try a little harder and, in President Hinckley's words, "stand a little taller."[1]

Excluding the Atonement, our purpose in coming to earth is the same as the Savior's. He was born to be a king. If faithful, we also are promised thrones, kingdoms, and principalities (see D&C 132:19). Jesus' kingdom was not of this world; neither is ours. In the Savior's response to Pilate, He stated that He was born to "bear witness unto the truth." We, too, were born and are reborn through the baptismal covenant to be a witness for the Truth, the Way, and the Life (see Mosiah 18:8–10).

Sister Bateman will first discuss the premortal world, foreordination, and the context it establishes for mortality.

Premortality and Foreordination (Sister Bateman)

A knowledge of the premortal life provides a framework for better understanding mortality. Prior to birth we were spirit children of a Heavenly Father. We had intellect, personality, talents, and agency. As personages of spirit it was possible for us to think and act independently. The scriptures indicate that the faithful spirits, those who accepted and lived the Father's plan, were chosen to be "added upon"; that is, to receive a physical body and to have experiences in a new earthly laboratory. The Lord told Abraham that those "who keep their first estate shall be added upon; . . . and they who keep their second estate [that is, mortality] shall have glory added upon their heads for ever and ever" (Abraham 3:26).

Not only did we exist as spirits before birth on this earth, but our faith and activities in premortality foreshadowed our opportunities and responsibilities here. Elder Russell M. Nelson has noted that women were promised special gifts "before the foundation of the world" so they could play a critical role in mortality. Quoting from the Doctrine and Covenants, Elder Nelson said:

Sisters received special gifts [before the foundation of the world]. They, according to the Lord, were empowered "to multiply and replenish the earth, according to my commandment, and to fulfil the promise which was given by my Father before the foundation of the world, . . . for their exaltation in the eternal worlds, that they may bear the souls of men; . . . herein is the work of my Father continued, that he may be glorified" (D&C 132:63). Think of it: When a mother bears and cares for a child, she not only helps the earth answer the end of its creation (D&C 49:16–17), but she glorifies God![2]

May I add that she also glorifies herself.

The same pattern of foreordination holds true for men. The prophet Alma taught that men who receive the holy priesthood were "called and prepared" in premortality. In Alma's words, righteous men were "called and prepared from the foundation of the world according to the foreknowledge of God, on account of their exceeding faith and good works; in the first place [that is, in premortality] being left to choose good or evil; therefore they having chosen good, and exercising exceedingly great faith, are called with a holy calling" (Alma 13:3).

I believe that men were not only foreordained to be priesthood holders but also were appointed to be husbands, fathers, and providers for their families.

All of us were in those councils, and we were assigned responsibilities commensurate with our faith. Speaking of the youth, President Gordon B. Hinckley has repeatedly stated that this is "the finest [and strongest] generation of young people ever in the history of this Church."[3] You were reserved for the last days when the earth would be in turmoil and confusion. I believe the Lord knew He could count on you to be an example, to live a righteous life, to stand as a witness for Him and His work.

It is important to understand that the principle of agency is eternal. It operated in premortality, it was preserved in the Fall of Adam, and it will continue to operate after death. Agency is a key to spiritual development. Righteous choices enhance our potential, whereas unwise choices lower the trajectory of our eternal path. The earth was created to be a learning laboratory for the body and the spirit. A veil drawn over our minds helps create this new laboratory (see 1 Corinthians 13:12). The veil separates us from the Lord, blanks our memory of the spirit world, and requires us to live by faith as we choose the paths we will follow. Spiritual development occurs when prayer draws us close to God and we choose to be obedient. Part of the earthly challenge is to pierce the veil, even in part, so that we may receive the Lord's guidance.

The Mortal Journey and Its Challenges (Sister Bateman)

As noted earlier, knowledge of the premortal world provides a context for mortality. This life is the second act of a three-act play. (It is possible to divide the eternal journey into more than three parts; however, for the purposes of this presentation, three have been chosen.) We lived before birth and we will continue to live after death. Although mortality is short, it is a very important portal through which we pass. It sets the compass for the path into the eternities.

There are three major purposes for the earth's creation and the mortal experience. The first is to obtain a physical body (see Abraham 3:26). The second is to grow spiritually by keeping the Lord's commandments (see Abraham 3:25). The third is to initiate an eternal family (see D&C 131:1–4; 132:19). Thus the physical body, spiritual growth, and family are the grand prizes of mortality.

The Physical Body and Its Challenges (Sister Bateman)

From birth to adulthood the body grows in strength and capability. For most people physical development peaks between twenty and thirty years of age, and then a long period of more or less steady deterioration follows. As you know, it matters a great deal whether we neglect our physical health or take care of and attend to the needs of the body. With proper care, a twenty-year-old can expect to reach eighty years of age or more,[4] a topic President Bateman will now discuss.

The Importance of Our Bodies (President Bateman)

The body is so important in the Lord's plan that He has given commandments and counsel in three areas. One commandment describes what is appropriate and what is not with respect to substances taken into the body. In every dispensation, from Adam to the present day, the Lord has revealed a health code. In this dispensation we call it the Word of Wisdom (see D&C 89). In addition to outlining proper foods for the body, the Lord commands that we abstain from alcohol, tobacco, and other harmful substances. These forbidden elements harm the body, reduce its capacity to perform, and shorten life. For example, research shows that smoking reduces life expectancy by thirteen to fourteen years.[5] The pattern of physical health associated with the consumption of alcohol, tobacco, and harmful drugs is the path of neglect.

Another law pertaining to the physical body is the moral code that prohibits sexual relations with anyone other than one's legally and lawfully married spouse. In our day the First Presidency and Quorum of the Twelve have stated:

> Physical intimacy between husband and wife is beautiful and sacred. It is ordained of God for the creation of children and for the expression of love between husband and wife. . . .
>
> When you obey God's commandment to be sexually pure, . . . you protect yourself from the emotional damage that always comes from sharing physical intimacies with someone outside of marriage.
>
> . . . Satan may tempt you to rationalize that sexual intimacy before marriage is acceptable when two people are in love. That is not true. In God's sight, sexual sins are extremely serious. . . . The prophet Alma taught that sexual sins are more serious than any other sins except murder or denying the Holy Ghost (see Alma 39:5).
>
> Before marriage, do not do anything to arouse the powerful emotions that must be expressed only in marriage. . . .
>
> . . . Always treat your date with respect, never as an object to be used for your lustful desires.[6]

Because of pride, Satan forfeited the opportunity to obtain a body. As a consequence, he will never be able to marry and have children. Though only a spiritual being, he retained a determination and the ability to use his considerable powers to oppose God's purposes. In his effort to deprive us of the joy that is the purpose of our existence (see 2 Nephi 2:25) and thwart the Lord's work—to provide each of us with immortality and eternal life (see Moses

1:39)—Satan has targeted our sacred power to procreate. In his unhappiness, he has vowed to do anything to disrupt the plan of happiness, which includes marriage and family.

A recent visitor on the BYU campus was reportedly stunned when he interviewed a number of students and learned that they voluntarily did not drink, smoke, use harmful drugs, or engage in sex outside of marriage. He was a police chief on another college campus who had come to review university security operations, and he could not believe what he had found here. He said the two major problems he sees on his campus daily are binge drinking and sexual abuse.

Another area of counsel in caring for the physical body concerns dress and grooming standards. Again, the First Presidency and Quorum of the Twelve have been very explicit in this area. I quote their words:

> Your body is God's sacred creation. . . . Through your dress and appearance, you can show the Lord that you know how precious your body is. . . .
>
> . . . The way you dress is a reflection of what you are on the inside. . . .
>
> Never lower your dress standards for any occasion. . . .
>
> Immodest clothing includes short shorts and skirts, tight clothing, shirts that do not cover the stomach, and other revealing attire. Young women should wear clothing that covers the shoulder and avoid clothing that is low-cut in the front or the back or revealing in any other manner. Young men should also maintain modesty in their appearance. All should avoid extremes in clothing, appearance, and hairstyle.[7]

There is a connection between how one dresses and one's appreciation of the physical body. I will return to this subject shortly.

Spiritual Progress and Its Challenges

Let us next consider the different trajectories that spiritual development may take. Again, the period from birth to adulthood can be a time of rapid growth. This is especially true for children born of goodly parents. Many of you, like Nephi and Enos, were raised in homes where parents set a good example, taught you to pray, and nurtured you in the admonition of the Lord. Some of you, on the other hand, are recent converts. You were contacted by the missionaries or had a friend introduce you to the gospel. Your spiritual understanding and growth may have come a few years later, but still early in life. And then there are many who do not find the gospel until late in life or even in the Millennium.

Spiritual development differs from the growth pattern for the physical body. It is not as time dependent. As long as one is obedient to eternal principles, the path has an upward slope. The height and steepness of the path are determined by the degree to which one adheres to God's laws.

There are many paths of spiritual development. It is possible to move from one path to another. Sin causes a shift to a lower trajectory, whereas an increase in faith and participation in covenants and ordinances allows one to move to a higher path.

All of us desire to be on the road leading to the celestial kingdom and eternal life. All of us experience challenges along the way. I will address three briefly. Meeting these challenges will help us prepare for eternal life.

The first challenge is to be fully committed. It is so easy to drift through life understanding what is important but only having a loose grasp on the iron rod. This is the "eat, drink, and be merry" syndrome. This is a satanic trap. In contrast, consider the commitment of a young marine in Vietnam in 1969 during the war. Elder Gordon B. Hinckley, then a member of the Twelve, visited Southeast Asia, where he met and interviewed a large number of LDS servicemen. He recalled:

[There I met] a handsome boy, tall, clean-faced, wholesome in his look. I said . . . , "What are you going to do when you go home? Have you ever thought of it?" . . .

. . ."Have I ever thought of it? I think of little else, sir. We're moving north again tomorrow, and if I can last another two months I know exactly what I'm going to do when I go home. I'm going to do three things. First, I'm going back to school and finish my education. . . .

"I'm also going to work in the Church and try to do some good. I've seen how desperately the world needs what the Church has to offer.

"And then I'm going to find me a beautiful girl and marry her forever."

Elder Hinckley countered with a question:

"Are you worthy of that kind of a girl?"

"I hope so, sir," he said. "It hasn't been easy to walk through this filth. It's been pretty lonely at times. But you know, I couldn't let my folks down. I know what my mother expects. I know what she's saying in her prayers. She'd rather have me come home dead than unclean." . . .

I don't know whether he lived or died. . . . We met and talked with so many and our schedule was so heavy that I do not recall his name or where he was from, but I have not forgotten him.[8]

The last days are not a time for casual commitments. The Lord needs young people firm in the faith to light the way. There are many in the world who would like what you have if they only knew where to find it. Don't miss the incredible opportunity to grasp the rod tightly and build a firm foundation that will bring happiness now and forever. The most important time in your life is now. Be fully committed.

The second challenge is to take care of the little things. Before becoming mayor of New York City, Rudolph Giuliani learned that if he paid attention to the little things, the big things often took care of themselves. Early in his administration he determined to eliminate graffiti throughout the city and also take care of the "squeegee man" problem. Giuliani believed that if so-called petty crime could be stopped, the effort would "establish lawful, civil behavior and a feeling of safety."[9] At the time "there were men who would step up to a car stopped at a red light or in traffic, spray the windshield, and wipe it down with a dirty rag." They were called "squeegee men." If the driver refused to pay them, car doors were kicked in or windows spat upon. Generally these shake-down artists chose to operate near the tunnels leading into or out of the city. Thus they created the first and last impressions for residents and visitors. Initially it was thought that there were thousands of these individuals. However, a careful survey revealed only about one hundred eighty. Steps were taken to enforce existing laws, and within a few days they were gone.[10] With the clampdown on these two minor problems, a remarkable thing happened: the number of murders and robberies in the city also fell.

The Family—A Prized Possession

The third purpose of mortality is to initiate an eternal family. Salvation is a one-by-one process, whereas exaltation is accomplished two-by-two and in family groupings. I am aware that not everyone has the opportunity to marry in this life. Fortunately, adjustments will be made in the Millennium for those who are worthy and do not have the opportunity here. The most important relationships in mortality—those of the family—are meant for eternity. A key witness of our belief in the eternal family is the construction of temples across the earth. A good part of temple work is associated with the family.

The creation of an eternal family requires the husband and wife to take the long view. Perfection does not come before the trial of faith. And marriage can be a trial of faith. It is important for a young man and a young woman to understand that love will deepen over time as each lives the principles of the gospel. The relationship between a man and a woman is designed to be eternal. Because the man and the woman are incomplete without each other, it is a complementary relationship. This is what Paul meant when he said, "Neither is the man without the woman, neither the woman without the man, in the Lord" (1 Corinthians 11:11). The relationship has the potential to refine and bring to fruition the spiritual gifts within each person. In taking the long view, family relationships through the power of the Holy Ghost can help family members put off the natural veneer and acquire the divine attributes. They become "submissive, meek, humble, patient, full of love" (Mosiah 3:19).

The world, however, is moving in the opposite direction. There are two tendencies. The first is to delay marriage. The second is to take marriage lightly. In the first case, more and more young people are waiting to marry until their late twenties. They want to complete their education and have a good job and a home and a car. Unfortunately, they will waste a significant portion of their productive lives.

The second tendency of not taking marriage seriously is reflected in the latest fad. Have you heard of the "starter marriage"? I guess it is like a starter home. It is a marriage that lasts no more than five years and has no children. It is the antithesis of the marriage called for in the eternal plan. It is a marriage with no faith, no hope, little meekness, and not much love. Can you imagine people finding happiness in such a circumstance? A challenge faced by society today is that people are looking for convenience and are unwilling to sacrifice. People have learned to discard everything from paper plates to spouses.

In closing, let us return to the three questions with which we began. Who are we? We are the spirit offspring of an Eternal Being who has given us the opportunity to experience mortality—a brief but critical time in an eternal journey. To what end were we born? We were born to become kings and queens with the power of life—with the power to initiate an eternal posterity. For this purpose we became stewards over a physical body and are given mortal challenges that allow us to grow. For what cause did we come? We came to be witnesses of the truth, to be good stewards, and to serve others and help them find the way.

It is my testimony that you were called and foreordained to lead God's work in these last days. Appreciate the grand prizes of mortality, be fully committed, take care of the little things, and have a view into the eternities. That is the road to peace (and happiness) in this life and eternal life in the world to come (see D&C 59:23).

NOTES

1. Gordon B. Hinckley, *Stand a Little Taller* (Salt Lake City: Eagle Gate, 2001).

2. Russell M. Nelson, "How Firm Our Foundation," *Ensign* 32 (May 2002): 75–76.

3. Gordon B. Hinckley, *Teachings of Gordon B. Hinckley* (Salt Lake City: Deseret Book, 1997), 714.

4. U.S. statistics indicate that a 20-year-old female's life expectancy is 80 years, whereas a male's is 75. Life expectancy for the LDS population exceeds the nation's because of lifestyle. See "United States Life Tables, 1999," *National Vital Statistics Reports* 50, no. 6 (21 March 2002): 4.

5. See National Center for Chronic Disease Prevention and Health Promotion report in "Annual Smoking—Attributable Mortality, Years of Potential Life Lost, and Economic Costs—United States, 1995–1999," *Morbidity and Mortality Weekly Report* 51, no. 14 (12 April 2002): 300–303.

6. *For the Strength of Youth* (Salt Lake City: Intellectual Reserve, Inc., 2001), 26–27.

7. *For the Strength of Youth,* 14–16.

8. Hinckley, *Teachings of Gordon B. Hinckley,* 710.

9. Rudolph W. Giuliani with Ken Kurson, *Leadership* (New York: Hyperion, 2002), 42.

10. Giuliani, *Leadership,* 41–43; see also 47–48.

LOOKING FORWARD

CHAPTER 17

The Dawn of a New Millennium

(11 JANUARY 2000)

THE DAWN OF a new millennium and the dusk of an old provide an opportunity to review key events and accomplishments of the recent past and ask what the future may hold. I realize that some believe the transition from one century and millennium to the next will occur at the end of the year 2000. For others the event has just taken place. Regardless of how one counts, we "stand on the summit of the ages." In the October 1999 general conference, President Gordon B. Hinckley spoke of standing "on the summit of the ages, awed by a great and solemn sense of history."[1] With eloquence he said: "What an exciting and wonderful thing it is to step across the threshold of the centuries. . . . Even more exciting is our opportunity to bridge the millennium that is drawing to a close and greet a new thousand years."[2] He continued:

> For some reason unknown to us, but in the wisdom of God, we have been privileged to come to earth in this

glorious age. There has been a great flowering of science. There has been a veritable explosion of learning. This is the greatest of all ages of human endeavor and human accomplishment. And more importantly, it is the season when God has spoken, when His Beloved Son has appeared, when the divine priesthood has been restored, when we hold in our hand another testament of the Son of God. What a glorious and wonderful day this is.[3]

There is an adage that says, "One does not see the future by looking in a rearview mirror." In contrast, there is another that declares: "Those who cannot remember the past are condemned to repeat it."[4] For a moment I wish to remind us of some of the spiritual and temporal high points since Joseph Smith's day and then look forward to the new century in anticipation of what lies ahead. We are fortunate to have prophets and apostles who are seers—servants who have provided us with a road map for the future. It is instructive to see what the Lord has said through them regarding the years ahead.

Some Highlights from the Last Two Centuries

Since the dawn of time, prophets have spoken of two special periods in the history of the earth. The first is the meridian of time, a time when the Son of God was born, ministered to His people, suffered death, and was resurrected. Moses, Samuel, Isaiah, Jeremiah, Zechariah, and numerous other prophets of the Old Testament foretold of this special season when the Son of God made the earth His footstool. It has now been 2,000 years since the Savior walked the earth, taught the gospel, healed the sick, raised the dead, and voluntarily gave His life that all of

His Father's children could have the opportunity to overcome physical and spiritual death.

The second special period referred to by the prophets is called the dispensation of the fulness of times. According to the Apostle Paul, it is an age when the Lord will "gather together in one all things in Christ, both which are in heaven, and which are on earth" (Ephesians 1:10; see also D&C 27:13). It is a period often referred to as the last days; a time just preceding the Lord's second coming; a time when He will restore the gospel to the earth, including all of the keys, powers, and authority previously bestowed in earlier days.[5]

Isaiah referred to the last days on numerous occasions. He foretold the establishment of the Lord's house "in the top of the mountains" and said that all nations would "flow unto it" (Isaiah 2:2). Isaiah also told of a people whose voice would speak from "the dust," whose words would be in the form of "a book that is sealed"—the words of which could not be read by learned men. And in that day, the Lord would proceed to do "a marvellous work and a wonder" (Isaiah 29:4, 11–12, 14).

Daniel foresaw a day when the Lord would set up a kingdom that would never be destroyed nor given to another people (see Daniel 2:44). The kingdom was represented by a "stone . . . cut out of the mountain without hands" that would roll across the earth, breaking in pieces earthly kingdoms (Daniel 2:45).

Malachi spoke of a day just before the Lord's second coming when Elijah the prophet would be sent to "turn the heart of the fathers to the children, and the heart of the children to their fathers, [lest the earth be smitten] with a curse" (Malachi 4:5–6).

Peter spoke of the last days when he told the Jews to repent before "the times of refreshing shall come from the presence of the Lord" and explained to them that Christ's second coming would not occur until "the times of restitution of all things" (Acts 3:19, 21). Finally, John the Revelator foretold of an event shortly before the Lord's second coming when an angel would return the everlasting gospel to the earth so that it could be preached "to every nation, and kindred, and tongue, and people" (Revelation 14:6).

The dispensation of the fulness of times represents a winding-up period preceding the coming of the Lord Jesus Christ. It is a time when the gospel will be preached to every nation, giving the Father's children an opportunity to prepare for the Son's second coming. It will be a day of judgment and the end of the world as we know it. The beginning of this dispensation was initiated by one of the greatest events in the course of human history—the appearance of the Father and Son to the boy Joseph Smith. To illustrate the majesty of the event in the Sacred Grove, can you think of another time when both the Father and the Son appeared on this earth? The scriptures tell of occasions when the Father's voice was heard from the heavens declaring His Only Begotten Son: for instance, at the Savior's baptism (Matthew 3:17), on the Mount of Transfiguration (Matthew 17:5), and to the Nephites in the land Bountiful (3 Nephi 11:3–7). But the Garden of Eden may be the only other place where both openly manifested Themselves on this earth.

Not only did the Father and the Son open the last dispensation, but John's angel proved to be Moroni, who restored the everlasting gospel so that it could be taken to every nation. The sealed plates Moroni revealed to Joseph Smith fulfilled Isaiah's prophecy that a people would speak out of the ground. The marvelous work and a wonder is the restoration of the gospel and the Book of Mormon's witness that Jesus is the Christ. Elijah returned the sealing keys to Joseph and Oliver Cowdery in the Kirtland Temple on 3 April 1836 (see D&C 110:14–16). Almost immediately the

Spirit of Elijah began stirring the hearts of men and women to gather family records and histories so that temple ordinances might be performed. Isaiah's "mountain of the Lord's house" (Isaiah 2:2) has been established in the tops of the mountains in the form of the Salt Lake Temple, and people from all nations have flowed to it both temporally and spiritually.

Peter's "times of refreshing" (Acts 3:19) refer to the fact that all knowledge that has ever been revealed plus knowledge reserved for the last days will come to light in this last dispensation. The Lord told Joseph Smith in Liberty Jail that no knowledge would be withheld, that "all thrones and dominions, principalities and powers" would be revealed, that the "bounds set to the heavens or to the seas, or to [the earth], or to the sun, moon, or stars—All the times of their revolutions . . . shall be revealed in the days of the dispensation of the fulness of times" (D&C 121:26–32). If one looks at the spiritual refreshing that has taken place through the prophets of this dispensation, plus the rapid discovery of temporal truths, can one doubt that the Lord is refreshing the earth, that the opportunity for men and women to be blessed both spiritually and temporally is vastly different today than at the turn of the 19th century?

To illustrate the change that has occurred, consider the field of transportation. From the beginning of time to the 19th century, the fastest mode of travel was the horse. Since the restoration of the gospel, new methods have been developed. Now we can travel on trains, automobiles, airplanes, and spaceships. Commercial air travel is so new that the first person ever to fly among my progenitors was my mother in 1947. Missionaries did not use air travel until the late 1950s. I left for England in 1956. The trip from Salt Lake City to London took ten days by train and ship. Two years later, when I returned home, travel by air was allowed.

It took just twenty-three hours to fly from Scotland to Salt Lake City with stopovers in Greenland, New York, and Chicago. The flight across the Atlantic was twelve hours, including the refueling stop in Greenland. Fifteen years later I flew from London to Washington, D. C., on the Concorde in just over three hours. Today a spaceship travels around the earth in little more than one hour.

Consider the innovations and discoveries of the last few years that influence everyday life: cellular telephones, computers, fax machines, the Internet, new medical devices and treatments, genetic engineering, robots, and the sequencing of the human genome, to mention but a few. The list is almost endless.

Unfortunately, the acceptance of temporal knowledge and its benefits has far exceeded the acceptance of spiritual truths. Although the gospel of peace is being taken to almost every corner of the earth, only a tiny fraction of the earth's population has accepted it. Nephi saw our day and said that the members of the Lord's Church would be small in number, but they would be "upon all the face of the earth" (1 Nephi 14:12). We are 12 million people today—less than one percent of the earth's population. We are scattered across the earth in more than 150 countries. The world has been slow to accept spiritual truths. "For the [20th] century as a whole, warfare is thought to have taken the lives of three times as many people as were killed in nineteen previous centuries combined."[6]

The 21st Century

What of the future? What are some of the key developments that will occur in the 21st century? What is the destiny of the Church as time rolls forward toward the Lord's second coming?

First, let us consider the missionary program. Today there are 12 million members and approximately 51,000 missionaries in more than 150 countries. By the year 2025, estimates suggest that Church population will total 25 million if China remains closed to missionary work and an even larger membership if China opens. Today slightly less than 50 percent of the Church membership resides in North America, with just under 40 percent in Central and South America. By the year 2025, Latin American membership will rise to 13 million (more than 50 percent), whereas Church population in North America will total 8 million. The missionary force in 2025 could reach 100,000. By 2025 the missionary program may be in every country with missionaries teaching every kindred, tongue, and people. The key variable that will determine the presence or absence of missionaries will be a nation's policies regarding religious freedom. Recent research indicates a strong movement toward freedom, especially in the last few years. A recent *Church News* article reported this progress as follows:

> Researchers found almost 60 percent of the world's population live in free societies, where basic rights and religious freedom flourish. . . . Freedom House—a pro-democracy group based in Washington, D.C.—remarked that whereas 100 years ago, no nation on earth had universal voting rights for its citizens, now 119 of 192 nations have elected representatives. The group could find only 18 nations in which civil liberties were suppressed last year by the military or their rulers.[7]

With newfound political freedom comes renewed hope that religious liberties are also gaining ground. The Apostle Paul in his epistle to the Corinthians wrote, "Where the spirit of the Lord is, there is liberty" (2 Corinthians 3:17).

David Gergen, editor-at-large of *U.S. News and World Report,* reported on this same research, indicating that "when the Berlin Wall fell a decade ago, 69 countries were democratic; last week the Freedom House reported the number has grown to 120."[8]

The trend toward freedom will continue during the 21st century. This will occur as the "stone . . . cut out of the mountain without hands" (Daniel 2:34) quietly, peacefully moves across the earth. It will occur so that the gospel message can be preached in all the world. Toward the end of Christ's life, His disciples, sitting with Him on the Mount of Olives, asked the following question: "Tell us when shall these things be . . . ; and what is the sign of thy coming, and of the end of the world?" (Joseph Smith—Matthew 1:4).

In response, Jesus told them He would come in a day when the elect would "be gathered from the four quarters of the earth"; a time "of wars, and rumors of wars"; a period in which there would "be famines, and pestilences, and earthquakes"; a time when "the love of men shall wax cold"; and a time when "this Gospel of the Kingdom shall be preached in all the world, for a witness unto all nations, and then shall the end come" (Joseph Smith—Matthew 1:27–31). Then Jesus reminded His disciples that no one knows the hour of His coming, not even the angels of heaven, but His Father only (see Joseph Smith—Matthew 1:40).

Although we do not know the exact time of the Lord's second coming, the signs of the times are gradually being fulfilled. We live in a day of wars and rumors of wars. Earthquakes are occurring with disturbing frequency. Famines dot the earth and invade parts of continents from one year to the next. An increasing divorce rate, the breakup of families, and larger and larger numbers of latchkey children are indicators that "the love of men [is] wax[ing] cold." The process of gathering the elect from the four corners of the earth has been underway for almost 170 years, and the number of countries enjoying the fruits of missionary work is approaching the full complement.

There are two other signs that clearly indicate the progress being made by the Church to take the gospel to the four corners of the earth. The first relates to family history and the influence of Elijah. The second relates to the increasing number of temples.

On 24 May 1999, the Church announced a new Web site for family history. The interest and activity on this site was phenomenal in the following seven months. Between 24 May and 30 December, the site experienced 2 billion hits. The site also has a free, downloadable version of the Personal Ancestral File software. More than 300,000 people have downloaded the software during the last few months. Literally millions of people across the earth have accessed the site. Daily traffic is running at a rate of 7 million hits per day. More than 5 million names have been uploaded to the file. The file now contains 600 million names in all.[9]

Can you imagine the progress that will be made during the next twenty-five years as members and nonmembers from almost every nation use the Internet to build family files and add to the names available for temple work? Family history is one of the most popular activities on the Internet and one of the leading avocations in the world. The Spirit of Elijah is alive and well. The developments in family history represent a miracle. No wonder the pace of temple construction has accelerated.

Now let me share a few thoughts regarding temples and their spread across the earth. Until recently, a phrase in an Isaiah passage dealing with the last days had escaped me. I have used

Isaiah 54:2 many times to explain how the Church grows. In this passage Isaiah likened the Church to a tent, using the Mosaic tabernacle as a metaphor. He described how the tent will spread over the earth by lengthening its cords and strengthening its stakes. Stakes in the Church are special units whose officers are given distinctive priesthood keys and authority to authorize saving and exalting ordinances. Church growth results in the establishment of new stakes.

Recently I noticed another phrase that has suddenly taken on meaning. In this same passage, Isaiah's instructions are to "enlarge the place of thy tent, . . . and stretch forth the curtains of thine habitations." I suddenly realized that the phrase "the curtains of thine habitations" refers to temples, to houses of the Lord. In looking at the last days, Isaiah saw that a key feature of Church growth would be the building of temples. Temples will spread across the earth. In fact, President Brigham Young said: "To accomplish this work there will have to be not only one temple but thousands of them, and thousands and tens of thousands of men and women will go into those temples and officiate for people who have lived as far back as the Lord shall reveal."[10]

For many years I thought President Young's statement would be fulfilled in the Millennium. Maybe it will, but it is incredible that we are living in a day when it has become apparent that thousands of temples will dot the earth. It is possible that there will be hundreds of temples by the year 2025, with hundreds more before you students pass through the veil. At the end of this year there will be at least 100 dedicated temples. If five temples per year are built during the coming 25 years, there would be over two hundred temples. That number is quite reasonable, considering there will be 35 or more temples dedicated this year.

I remember a meeting of the General Authorities in March

1997. The Church was preparing to dedicate its 50th operating temple after 167 years of this dispensation. At the end of the meeting, President Gordon B. Hinckley stated that he hoped there would be at least 100 temples operating before he completed his assignment on earth. I sat there stunned. The president was in his 87th year. It had taken 167 years for the first 50 temples to be built. I knew him to be an optimistic man, but how could another 50 temples be built in the remaining years of his ministry?

A few months later, in another meeting, President Hinckley announced the concept of the small temple. On a long summer trip, returning from the old Mormon colonies in Mexico, the manner in which these temples should be constructed was revealed to him. The temples would be of the same quality as the larger ones, they would be built of the finest materials, and they would be constructed to last for hundreds of years. Moreover, many of them would be built next to existing stake centers. What has followed is a miracle as the Lord through his prophet is stretching "the curtains of [His] habitations" across the earth (3 Nephi 22:2).

Do you understand the importance of temples in the Lord's plan? Do you understand how important it is to be worthy of entering a temple? Do you realize that temple work will be a key activity in the Millennium? It is clear that the Lord is preparing the earth for His second coming. May we appreciate the day in which we live. Our pioneer ancestors sacrificed everything they had in order that we might see this day. May we live each day as if the Lord had already come.

NOTES

1. Gordon B. Hinckley, "At the Summit of the Ages," *Ensign* 29 (November 1999): 74.

2. Hinckley, "At the Summit of the Ages," 72.

3. Hinckley, "At the Summit of the Ages," 74.

4. George Santayana, "Flux and Constancy in Human Nature," in *Reason in Common Sense,* vol. 1 of *The Life of Reason* (New York: Charles Scribner's Sons, 1905–1906), 284.

5. See Bruce R. McConkie, *Mormon Doctrine,* 2nd ed., rev. (Salt Lake City: Bookcraft, 1966), 200, s.v. "dispensation of the fulness of times."

6. David Gergen, "Roaring into 2000," *U.S. News and World Report* 128, no. 1 (3–10 January 2000): 96.

7. Viewpoint, "Blessing of Liberty," *Church News,* 8 January 2000, 16.

8. Gergen, "Roaring into 2000," 96.

9. Data from Richard E. Turley, managing director of the Church's Family History Department.

10. Brigham Young, in *Journal of Discourses,* 26 vols. (Liverpool: F. D. Richards, 1855–86), 3:372, 22 June 1856.

CHAPTER 18

The Challenges of
the 21st Century

(26 AUGUST 2002)

Each year I approach this assignment with some apprehension because I believe the Annual University Conference is one of the most important events of the year. It is an opportunity for the faculty, staff, and administration of Brigham Young University to gather together and reset our course, to orient our compasses. Since the university's journey began well before we entered the scene and will continue long after we are gone, the directions set in these meetings are critical for us and for those who follow. This is also a time for new associates to begin the orientation process at this unique institution. A perceptive person soon learns that orientation is not a one-week or one-year activity but that it takes years to appreciate fully the university's mission and to see how one may best contribute. The conference is also a time to recognize the achievements of various faculty and staff.

During last year's Annual University Conference, five

challenges and opportunities were presented.[1] They included the following:

- building a university community
- continuous reinvention
- focusing resources
- mentored student learning, and
- continual curriculum improvement.

My purpose today is not to issue new challenges but to provide a perspective on what lies ahead and encourage us to recommit to the opportunities just mentioned, especially in light of an ever-improving student body, continual faculty and staff turnover, new technology, and increasing donor support to our efforts.

Building a University Community

First, may I address the opportunity we have to build on the legacy of a strong community. I believe that the most important lesson learned from 11 September 2001 concerns the blessings that come in being part of a strong community. Sabotaged airliners crashing into the World Trade Center and into the Pentagon did not fracture the American psyche or produce a crushing fear in the hearts of the people because the common beliefs shared by Americans were a unifying force that drew us close together and gave us the strength to carry on. Americans became even more determined to protect our freedoms and stand against terrorism. I am reminded of the Nephites, who banded together "to support their lands, and their houses, and their wives, and their children, that they might preserve them from the hands of their enemies; and also that they might preserve their rights and their privileges, yea, and also their liberty" (Alma 43:9). America rallied from New York in the east to California and Hawaii in the west in support of those who suffered most from the terrible events. We came closer together as a nation, willing to root out those with their secret combinations who would try to destroy our way of life. The enemy—a small band living in the wilderness and performing their terrorist acts in the cities of the world—would no longer be allowed to roam freely across the earth (see Helaman 2:11 and 3:23 for a close parallel).

Just as the principles of freedom have united America since 9/11, so does a common faith unite our community of higher learning. Brigham Young University is more than the sum of its individual parts. Generally the quality of a university is determined by summing the reputations of the faculty and staff. Faculty and staff accomplishments play a key role at BYU as well. But there is a force far beyond individual strengths that defines this institution. That force, the institution's greatest asset, is the common faith that binds us together and that defines the university as part of the Lord's kingdom and an integral part of His Church.

Teaching by the Spirit

For some time I have thought about Brigham Young's challenge to Karl Maeser that every subject be taught under the influence of the Spirit.[2] What did he mean by this? I have generally understood that the instructor should be worthy of the promptings that come from the Holy Ghost, and the student likewise. This is consistent with the Lord's instructions to Joseph Smith in D&C 50. With a little license, verses 21 and 22 read as follows: "Therefore, why is it that ye cannot understand and know, that he that receiveth the word by the Spirit of truth receiveth it as it is [taught] by the Spirit of truth? Wherefore, he that [teaches] and he that [receives], understand one another, and both are edified and rejoice together" (D&C 50:21–22).

Is that the sum total of what President Young was asking Brother Maeser to do? Was his directive fulfilled by having the Holy Ghost's influence as a teacher and guide? If so, learning at this institution would be accelerated and the discovery of truth would be enhanced. I suspect, however, that the prophet would not be satisfied if Brother Maeser and those who followed him were to use only one of the gifts available through the Holy Spirit. Yes, the Holy Ghost is a great teacher and will lead us to truth. But there are many gifts that He is willing to share with those who are prepared and seek after them (see D&C 46:8).

For example, do we as faculty and staff seek the gift of discernment to know what our students comprehend and what they do not? Have you suddenly become aware of a particular student and realized that he or she missed a key point? I will never forget sitting on the stand as a bishop in a fast and testimony meeting. As I looked out over the congregation, I suddenly knew what a number of individuals were thinking as they listened to the testimonies. I could tell which members needed help and the nature of the problems they faced. Is it appropriate for a faculty member at Brigham Young University to enjoy this same power? Why not? The teacher with this gift senses the impact of his or her teaching and is able to assess what should be done to enhance student understanding. The gift allows one to tailor the help for each individual and to create more effective ways of communicating. Elder Maxwell often speaks of the Lord's ability to tailor lessons to each person's needs. I am convinced that the Lord will share this power with us if we seek after it. He will do so because our intent is to bless others.

What about the gift of love? This power is a fruit of the Spirit (see Galatians 5:22). Do we ask the Lord to bless us with a special care and concern for those whom we teach? I know from personal experience that one becomes a more effective teacher when he or she has strong, positive feelings toward those being taught. Can you imagine the impact of a missionary who is indifferent to or even dislikes the investigators? Worthy missionaries are blessed in due course with a special gift of love for those they are called to serve. As a stake president I interviewed a large number of young men and women returning from the field. I could tell in a very short time how effective they had been as teachers by the feelings they had for the people. Is our calling to teach 30,000 young Church members any less significant? I believe we are entitled to this fruit, and our effectiveness depends on it. Without it we may instruct, but we will never edify!

Finally, I pray that each of us will have the gift of wisdom— even above the gift of knowledge. I pray that we will be wise in our relationships with students, that we will be sensitive to the trust that has been placed in us to nurture their testimonies. I hope we will be wise in using the resources made available to us. They are the consecrations of the Saints and include the widow's mite. May we have wisdom as we meet members whose children are not able to study with us. May we be wise in seeking ways for BYU to bless all members of the Church. May we have the wisdom to appreciate the incredible future of this university and the great opportunity and blessing it is to be a part of it. I love and appreciate you, brothers and sisters. I plead with the Lord daily for the wisdom and faith necessary to lead His university. May all of us commit to the destiny of this institution is my prayer.

NOTES

1. Merrill J. Bateman, "The Banyan Tree" (paper presented at the Annual University Conference, Brigham Young University, 27 August 2001).

2. See Alma P. Burton, *Karl G. Maeser: Mormon Educator* (Salt Lake City: Deseret Book, 1953), 26.

EPILOGUE

Farewell Address

(18 MARCH 2003)

First, may I pay tribute to my wife, Marilyn. She has been faithful to the Lord all her life and loyal to me for more than four decades. She is sensitive to the Spirit and wise in her judgment. She has raised seven children and is now grandmother to twenty-eight. She is as interested in the grandchildrens' development as she was with her childrens'. Her sacrifices have paved the trail of our mortality. I love her with all my heart. I love you with all my heart.

Almost seven and one-half years ago I received a call from President Hinckley's office asking if I could attend a meeting in the First Presidency's boardroom. The purpose was not made known. As I entered the hallway leading to the appointed place, President Faust entered as well and it was apparent that we were headed in the same direction. I asked if he would be in the meeting to which I had been called. He said, "Yes!" About that time I began to have a sinking feeling. I wondered what I had done. As the recently appointed Presiding Bishop, was there special counsel that I needed? Little did I know the change in direction that was about to take place. Little did I understand the great opportunity that lay ahead for Marilyn and me.

As we entered the room, President Hinckley and President Monson were already there. It soon became apparent that the meeting was with the First Presidency, and I was the only guest. It was not long before President Hinckley asked if I would accept a change in assignment and become the eleventh president of Brigham Young University. Although I remember saying that I would do whatever they asked, I was stunned. Marilyn and I had lived next door to Rex and Janet Lee for twenty years. We knew that President Lee was very ill, but never assumed that we might be asked to take their place.

The seven years that followed have been among the richest of our lives. We have come to love the faculty, staff, and students more than we dreamed possible. Over many years I have learned that the Lord blesses those who serve Him with a special gift, the gift of love for those whom they serve. This is true for a missionary, a bishop, a Relief Society president, a stake president. And I know now it is true for the president of BYU.

As the years have gone by, we have come to know hundreds of faculty and staff and thousands of students. We have noticed the light within you, as have numerous visitors to campus. I will always remember the Argentine ambassador asking if all the buildings are new, how we keep the campus so clean, why the students are so happy, and what is the special light in your eyes. Nor will I forget another diplomat who suggested an experiment. If he were to bring students to this campus from another university he had visited, would they eventually look like you?

We know the Lord has gathered you from the four corners of the earth for a special purpose. You come from 120 countries, speak more than 70 languages. Your purpose in coming is to increase both intellectually and spiritually and then spread across the earth establishing righteous homes, raising faithful children, and giving service to others. Several years ago I attended a branch of the Church in Beijing, China. At the time, all of the members were expatriates, mostly American. Most were employed in multinational firms in high positions. Approximately fifty families were in attendance. During the priesthood meeting, I asked who had served Chinese-speaking missions. All but three raised their hands. I then asked how many were BYU graduates. Again, a large majority were alumni. The impression came that they were pioneers. They were in the Lord's hands and were preparing the way.

I believe the Lord has a mission for you. That is why you as faculty, staff, and students are here. Just as I did not foresee my role as president of BYU, neither will you anticipate all that lies ahead. But be assured: the Lord knows your name, He knows the righteous desires of your hearts, and He desires your help in establishing His kingdom on this earth. You may not find yourself in a foreign outpost, but your efforts to build a righteous family and serve your neighbors will save not only others but your own family. He asks that you walk by faith, take a step into the unknown. He will be your guide.

BYU is an extraordinary academic institution, but its uniqueness among all major universities lies in its spiritual dimension. Teaching and research under the guidance of the Holy Spirit enhances learning. This university is rapidly becoming one of the finest educational institutions in the country. Along with President John Taylor and others, I have seen the day when this institution will lead in all fields of knowledge because its people will be of one heart and one mind and there will be no intellectually or spiritually poor among them. May the Lord bless Elder and Sister Samuelson and all of you as you work together to achieve this end is my prayer in the name of Jesus Christ. Amen.

Index

21st century, 246–51

Abraham: desires knowledge, 29–30;
    covenant with, 82–84; promised
    land and, 101–2; promised son,
    102–4
Absolutism, 41–42
Academic freedom: at Brigham Young
    University, 22–24; search for truth
    and, 38–41; challenges to, 41–43
Adam and Eve, desire knowledge, 29
Adversity: having faith in face of, 98;
    having courage in face of, 116–19
Africa, growth of Church in, 14–16
Agency, 229; obedience and, 40–41; in
    premortal existence, 196
Alcohol, 113–14
America: Harold B. Lee on, 222; unites
    after September 11, 2001, 254–55
"Am I Beautiful to You?" 129
Angioplasty, 150–51
Aristotle, on knowledge, 30
Atonement, 190–91; author's testimony
    of, 91–92; as choice, 165–66;
    ordinances of, 167–70; Margaret

Wahlstrom on having testimony
    of, 174; bodies and, 178–80

Baptism, 167–68
Baseball, 204–7
Baseball glove, 174
Bateman, Marilyn, dream of, 216–18
Bateman, Michael, 204–7
Belief, 124–25
Bethesda, healing at, 168–70
Bible, 16–17, 83
Binge drinking, 113–14
Black, Susan Easton, 74
Blessing LDS members, as Brigham
    Young University's third objective,
    73–75
Blessings: of testimony, 110–19; father's,
    204–7
Body: sacredness of, 113; as temple,
    178–80; temptations of, 197;
    purity and, 219–20; importance
    of, 230–33
Bohr, Niels, Arthur Henry King on,
    20–21
Bradford, Reed, 62

Brazil: growth of Church in, 14; Internet courses in, 74–75

Brazilian graduate student, 109–10

Brimhall, George, on Karl G. Maeser, 61

Burton, Alma, 62

Brigham Young University: mission of, ix–x, 46–48; relationship to Church of, 17–19; as Zion university, 19–22; faculty responsibility and academic freedom in, 22–24, 41–43; importance of students of, 24–26; search for truth at, 35–38; students of, as children of the covenant, 48–53; beginning of, 56–57; from 1875–1900, 58–62; from 1900–1950, 62–65; from 1951–1971, 65–66; from 1971–1999, 67; institutional objectives of, 68–77; future of, 77–78; as Lord's garner, 112–14; Honor Code of, 130–31; Light of Christ and, 148; tolerance at, 172; as temple of learning, 175–78; doors are opened for girl to attend, 185–87; Merrill Bateman called as President of, 259–60; uniqueness of, 261–62

Cana, 166–67

Canaan, 101–2

Cannon, James W., receives answer through Holy Ghost, 21

Chemotherapy, 151–52

Children, 202

Children of the covenant, Brigham Young University students as, 48–53

Children with disabilities, 72

China, members as pioneers in, 261

Church of Jesus Christ of Latter-day Saints, The: worldwide growth of, 13–18; relationship of Brigham Young University to, 17–19;

Brigham Young University as window for, 77–78; future of, 246–51

Clark, Harold Glen, 62

Clark, Harold R., 62

Cleanliness, 24–25

Cluff, Benjamin Jr., 61–62

Commandment, to learn, 33–34

Configurable computing, 73

Courage, 116–19

Covenant: children of, 48–53; people, 82–84

Cowdery, Oliver, 85–86

Dant, Doris, on great building, 211

Decisions, 210–11

de Jong, Gerrit, 62

Depression, development of test to measure, 72–73

Deseret, University of, 19

Diligence, 32–33, 84–91

Dispensation of the fullness of times, 243–46

Divinity, 198–99

Dream, 148–53; of Karl G. Maeser, 59–60, 178; of Marilyn Bateman, 216–18

Drinking, 113–14

Dusenberry, Warren, 58–59, 61

Education: importance of, 109–10; of Jesus Christ, 157–62

Eduok, Ime, 15–16

Edwards, Deanna, 129

Eight-year-olds, author called to teach, 149–50

Employment, effect of Internet courses on, 75

England, 13–14

Enrollment, expanding, 73

Eyring, Carl, 62

Faculty: of Brigham Young University, 22–24; survey on, sharing gospel, 68–69; wants to help students, 187–88

Faith, 124–27; as process for learning, xii, 221–22, Joseph Smith on, 33, 86; as principle of gospel, 97–99; Paul and, 99–101; obedience and, 132-33; growth of Jesus Christ's, 157–62; in mortality, 197

Family: eternal, xiv–xv, 196–98; effect of Brigham Young University on, 70; children with disabilities and, 72; as central part of plan of salvation, 201–3; building successful, 203–8; affect of terrorism on, 209–10; building eternal, 212–18; as purpose of life, 236–37

Family history, 249

"Family, The: A Proclamation to the World," 23–24, 199–201

Father, of Marilyn Bateman, 216–18

Father's blessings, 204–7

Faust, James E., on secularization of Brigham Young University, ix

Figuerres, Cyril, 122, 136–38

First Presidency: on physical intimacy, 231; on modesty, 232

First Vision, 86–91

Fletcher, Harvey, 62

Foreordination, 227–29

Freedom, 247–49; Neal A. Maxwell on, 40–41

Freshman, finds way to attend Brigham Young University, 185–87

Friends: gaining, as Brigham Young University's fourth objective, 76; companionship of good, 114–16

Future, 246–51

Gadianton robbers, 209

Garner, 112–13

Gergen, David, on free countries, 248

Giuliani, Rudolph, 235

Glasses, 114–16

Glutaric acidemia, 104–8

God: omniscience of, 30–32; Jesus Christ's relationship with, 159, 164

Gospel, xiv; Brigham Young on science and, 18; survey on professors sharing, 68–69; light of, 81–82; faith as principle of, 97–99; introductory ordinances of, 167–70; as answer to terrorism, 172–73

Graffiti, 235

Granary, 112–13

Grandchildren, 218

Grant, Heber J., 63–65

Great Britain, growth of Church in, 13–14

Great Depression, effect on Brigham Young University of, 63–65

Hafen, Bruce C., on hireling versus shepherd, 203

Harris, Franklin S., 63

Healing, at Bethesda, 168–70

Health code, 230

Heart surgery, 150–51

Heather, 104–8

Heavenly Father: Jesus Christ's relationship with, 159, 164; Jesus Christ as only begotten of, 165

Hinckley, Gordon B.: on faculty of Brigham Young University, 50–51; on Proclamation, 199–200; on being weak link in family, 218; on youth, 228; on marine in Vietnam, 234–35; on millennium, 241–42; announces small temples, 251

Hispanic woman, knows life has purpose, 195–96

Holland, Jeffrey R.: visits Brigham Young University campus, 77–78; on moral purity, 219–20

Holy Ghost: learning with, 20–22; receiving witness of, 99–101; as key in relationship with God, 133–35; teaches girl in physics class, 149; gaining fullness of, 159; teaching with, 255–57

Honor, 193

Honor Code, 130–31

Hope, 116–19, 139–41

Immoral acts, 113

Incoherence of the Philosophers, The, 77

Intelligence, 31; Brigham Young on purpose of, 34; purpose of, 195–96, 226–27; marriage and family as purpose of, 236–37. *See also* Knowledge

Internet: learning through, 73–75; family history and, 249

Isaac, 102–4

Japan: author finds man in, 81–82; missionaries help after storm in, 122–24, 136–38

Japanese man, understands need for Savior, 114–16

Japanese woman, knows Jesus Christ loves her, 193–94

Jesus Christ, 135–36; learning of, xiii–xiv, 31–32; gospel of, xiv; light of, 34–35, 164–65; author's testimony of, 91–92; faith in, 97–99, 126–27; Abraham's faith in, 103–4; handicapped girl has faith in, 104–8; Japanese man understands need for, 114–16; second coming of, 121, 248–49; obedience of, 132–33; love of, 127–30; serving with love of, 136–38; at Last Supper, 140–41; as infinite source of all power, 149; teaches at temples, 155–56; spiritual growth of, 157–62; relationship with Father of, 164, 165; as Lamb of God, 166; Atonement and, 165–66, 190–91; mission of, 166–67, 226; building one by one relationship with, 188–90; coming unto, 191–93

Kane, Thomas L., letter to Brigham Young from, 58

Kimball, Spencer W.: on Brigham Young University, 37; on search for truth at Brigham Young University, 37; on service, 215–16

Kinder, Joan, 117–19

King, Arthur Henry, on Niels Bohr and discovering truths, 20–21

Knight, Jesse, 62–63

Knowledge: quest for, 29–30; acquiring, 32–35; seeking, 176

Lamb of God, 166

Larson, Clinton, 62

Last days, 243–46

Last Supper, 140–41

Law, obedience to higher, 130–32

Laycock, Douglas, on secular absolutism, 41–42

LDS members, blessing, as Brigham Young University's third objective, 73–75

Learning: John Taylor on, x; of Jesus Christ, xiii–xiv, 31–32, 157–62; in new millennium, xv; with Holy Ghost, 20–22; principles of, 32–35; process for, 84–91; Brigham Young University as temple of, 175–78; by study and faith, 221–22; in last days, 245–46

Lee, Harold B.: on Brigham Young University's role in prophecy, 67; on America, 222

"Lehi's Dream," 211–16

Letter: on Brigham Young Unversity's students, 49–50; from Thomas L. Kane to Brigham Young, 58

Light, xiii; discovering, 32–35; of Christ, 34–35, 164–65; of gospel, 81–82; physical and spiritual, 146–48; in Brigham Young University students, 260–61

Little League, 204–7

Loneliness, 187–88

Love: as motive, 127–30; for students,
256–57

Maeser, Karl G.: Brigham Young's
charge to, 56; role in Brigham
Young Academy of, 59–61; has
dream of Brigham Young
University, 178
Marine, 234–35
Marriage, 200–201, 236–37; feast at
Cana, 166–67
Marriott Center, 177–78
Martin, Thomas, 62
Maxwell, Neal A.: on God's knowledge,
31; on obedience and freedom,
40–41; on Ernest L. Wilkinson, 66
McConkie, Bruce R., on faith, 133
McKay, David O., on parenting, 202
Medical advancements, 150–52
Men: and women, 198–99; promised
special gifts, 228
Meridian of time, 242–43
Mexico: Internet courses in, 74–75;
missionary gains testimony of First
Vision in, 86–91
Micro-electro-mechanical systems, 152
Millennium, progress in new, xv, 55. *See
also* Last days
Miracles, 15–17
Mission: of Brigham Young University,
46–48; of Jesus Christ, 166–67,
226
Missionaries: employing returned, 75;
gains testimony of First Vision,
86–91; help after tropical storm in
Japan, 122–24, 136–38
Missionary program, future of, 246–47
Modesty, 232
Money, Brigham Young University's
early lack of, 56
Mortality, 196–98: Brigham Young on
purpose of, 34; purpose of,
226–27; challenges of, 229–30
Motto, 124

Nelson, Russell M.: on growth of
Church in Russia, 16–17; on
women's special gifts, 227–28
Nephites, 188–90
New Testament, 163–64
New York City, 235
Nibley, Hugh, 62
Nigeria, author finds Ime Eduok in,
15–16

Oaks, Dallin H.: on covenant, 48–53;
on Ernest L. Wilkinson, 66; on
objectives for Brigham Young
University, 67
Obedience: to laws, 33; agency and,
40–41; learning by, 84–91; to
gospel principles, 130–33
Omniscience, 30–32
One by one relationship, 188–90
Only Begotten Son, 165
Open-heart surgery, 150–51
Ordinances: of Atonement, 167–70;
administered one by one, 190

Painting, 213–16
Palmyra Temple, 177–78
Paul, faith and, 99–101
Peace, 139–41
Peculiar treasure, 83–84
Penrose, Charles W., xiii; on Light of
Christ, 147–48
Physical intimacy, 231–32
Physics class, 149
Pioneers, members in China as, 261
Pitt, William, 151–52
Plan of salvation: testimony of, 116–19;
premortal existence and, 196;
eternal families and, 196–98;
family as central part of, 201–3
Policeman, 173–74
Pontius Pilate, 226
Pornography, 180
Prayer: Jesus Christ taught, 158–59;
coming unto Jesus Christ through,
192

Premortal existence, 196, 227–29
Priesthood, foreordination of, 228
Procreative power, 196, 219–20, 231–32
Progress, xv; scientific, 145–46; of Jesus Christ, 157–62; spiritual, 233–35; in last days, 245–46
Promised land, 101–2
Protection, 111–14
Provo Temple, 64–65
Purity, 219–20

Quiz, Russian professor rocks baby during, 70

Research, 71–73
Respect, 193
Resurrection, 168–70
Revelation, 148–49, 162–63
Ricks College, 63
Russia, growth of Church in, 16–17
Russian professor, rocks baby during quiz, 70
Russian woman, prays for Bible, 16–17

Santiago, Tessa Meyer, on Zion, 53
Savior, Japanese man understands need for, 114–16
School of the Prophets, 18
Science, Brigham Young on gospel and, 18
Scientific discoveries, 145–46
Scott, Richard G., on faith in Jesus Christ, 98
Scriptures: author gains testimony of, 149–50; Jesus Christ's study of, 159–61; importance of studying, 162–70; coming unto Jesus Christ through, 192–93
Second Coming, 121, 248–49
Secular absolutism, 41–42
Secularization, ix–x
September 11, 2001, xii–xiii, 171–75; devotional given on, 139–41; America unites after, 254–55

Service, 122–24, 136–38; Spencer W. Kimball on, 215–16
Sexual discipline, 113, 219–20, 231–32
Small temples, 251
Smith, Joseph: on School of the Prophets, 18; on faith, 33, 125; on working by faith, 86; changes Paul's definition of faith, 99; on revelation, 148–49; last days and, 244
Smoot, Abraham O., 59, 61
Son, Abraham promised, 102–4
Songs, 104–8
Sperry, Sidney B., 62, 63–65
Spiritual growth, 157–62, 233–35
Squeegee men, 235
Stakes: in Great Britain, 13–14; Church growth and, 250
Stone, Elder, 86–91
Stone, Lawrence, on marriage, 199–200
Storm, 122–24, 136–38
Strength, in face of adversity, 116–19
Student(s): importance of Brigham Young University's, 24–26; as children of the covenant, 48–53; from Brazil learns importance of education, 109–10; Honor Code and, 130–31; faculty wants to help, 187–88; love for, 256–57; light in, 260–61
Study, learning by, 221–22
Sumiya, Mitsunori, 136–38
Sunday school, author called to teach, 149–50
Surgery, 150–51
Survey: on statistics of college students, 51–52; on professors sharing gospel, 68–69
Synoptic Gospels, 163–64

Taylor, John: on learning and Zion, x; on advancement of Zion, 37; has vision of Brigham Young, 47
Teaching: with testimony, 20; Brigham Young on, 56; as Brigham Young

University's first objective, 68–71; with Holy Ghost, 255–57

Teichert, Minerva, 211–16

Temple: Sidney B. Sperry has vision of Provo, 64–65; as Lord's garner, 112; Jesus Christ teaches at, 155–56; Brigham Young University as, 175–78; bodies as, 178–80; Church growth and, 249–51

Temptation: of body, 197; avoiding, 221–22

Terrorism, 209–10

Testimony: teaching with, 20; gaining, 86–91, 99–101; of author, 91–92; blessings of, 110–19; Margaret Wahlstrom on, 174

"There Is Sunshine in My Soul Today," 104–8

Tolerance, 172

Traditions, 203–8

Tragedy, 117–19

Transportation, 245–46

Trials, 98, 117–19

Tropical storm, 122–24, 136–38

Truth: search for, 32–38; academic freedom and search for, 38–41

Typewriters, 150

University of Deseret, 19

Veil, 229

Vietnam, 234–35

Visions, 148–53

Wahlstrom, Margaret, on having testimony of Atonement, 174

Water: turned into wine, 166–67; ordinances and, 167–68

Welch, John, on great building, 211

West Africa, growth of Church in, 14

Wilkinson, Ernest L., 66

Williams, Zina Young, 47

Wilson, Keith, 68–69

Wine, 166–67

Wisdom, 257

Witness, receiving, 99–101

Women: and men, 198–99; promised special gifts, 227–28

Word of Wisdom, 113–14, 230

Young, Brigham: on science and gospel, 18; on purpose of mortality, 34; John Taylor has vision of, 47; on teaching, 56; establishes Brigham Young Academy, 58–62; promised land and, 102; on temples and Church growth, 250

Youth, Gordon B. Hinckley on, 228

Zion: John Taylor on, x, 37; Tessa Meyer Santiago on, 53

Zion university, 19–22